400 Court Street presents

The History of Professional Wrestling in Evansville, IN: 1959

Adapted from the 400 Court Street podcast

by Sean Dulaney

First Printing: September 2020

Sean Dulaney/BiMor Press
P.O. Box 7
New Haven, IL   62867

Press inquiries can be sent to b1morcomics@bspeedy.com

TABLE OF CONTENTS

PREFACE: Why Start In 1959...?

A very valid question. To be honest, it was totally by accident. I launched the *400 Court Street* program/podcast due, in part, to the majority of the Memphis territory *Championship Wrestling* shows on YouTube were the Evansville versions taped from WTVW-7 and included the local promo interviews for the Coliseum shows. But as I started doing research, I discovered Evansville's wrestling history was so much more than what the Jarretts brought to town in the 70s. I discovered a ban on professional matches born from the first World's Championship meeting between Strangler Lewis and Joe Stecher. I learned of promotional wars that ranged from former partners to fraternal organizations to the Jarrett/Poffo feud fought mostly in the towns surrounding Evansville. I found the down years after the Korean War and the boom that saw Evansville part of a tug-of-war between NWA offices, only to be shuttered for almost a decade for circumstances beyond local fans' control.

Something that helped me take the show beyond the Memphis crew was discovering a series of message board posts giving Evansville results that had been compiled by historians Steve Yohe and Don Luce. After finding all the posts and putting them in chronological order, I thought I had a solid starting point to do the show.

The series of shows covering 1959 was going to be one, maybe two shows running through results and going deeper of some of the talents that came through the area, having already produced an episode spotlighting Rip Hawk. (1959 selected for the spotlight due to the number of national stars who appeared at the Coliseum that year.) But at the exact same time, I discovered the Evansville-Vanderburgh Public Library had added the complete *Evansville Press* to their digital archives, and found that the Press would often go much deeper into their coverage of the local wrestling office than the *Courier*.

So, one show turned into a 6-part series with a bonus show for corrections… And now, a book adapted from the scripts/essays I wrote for the shows. If you picked this up because you're a wrestling history fan or a student of Evansville's history, I hope you enjoy what we've put together.

Sean Dulaney
September 25, 2019

December 1958-January 1959

1959 was a study in contrasts. The post-War boom was in decline but there was growth in other sectors. The homefront idealism that got us through WW2 was giving way to a certain cynicism born on the battlefield. Rather than all pulling together, people started to suspect everyone else had an angle. But within a year, the children who had been too young to fight in the 40s and the children who were born right after the war ended started embracing the promise of a "New Frontier."

Locally, annexation plans that grew the city to the North and East were revealed and put in motion. A new museum building on the riverfront would open, Evansville College would be the country's hottest team in their division and Rex Mundi would unveil its first basketball team, but that's later in the year.

In 1959, pro wrestling on national television was as dead as the DuMont Network. But like many promoters in other cities, the local promoter Leon Balkin had started his own show in 1956. On Saturday nights at 10pm, WTVW was home to live *Studio Wrestling* broadcasts, featuring the stars working for Leon Balkin Wednesday nights at the Coliseum. Due to Evansville's proximity to the cities, Balkin had partnered with both the Nashville booking office run by Nick Gulas and Roy Welch and the Central States/St Louis Wrestling Club controlled by NWA president Sam Muchnick to provide talent for his Wednesday cards and Saturday night TV. Unfortunately, business going into December of 1958 was down and had been for some time. A card with the NWA Champion at the brand new Roberts Municipal Stadium in 1957 would draw only 1,800 people. Advance ticket sales on Wednesdays were in the teens and twenties on a good night and the walk-up business would be hit and miss, but Balkin soldiered on.

Because he had a live weekly TV show, a lot of the things Leon had done in the past fell by the wayside, specifically going dark in the summer months due to the Coliseum turning into a sweatbox. But being a family man, he did still suspend the weekly cards over the holidays following the 1958 Courier Christmas Fund event in mid-December, using his Saturday night show to build for the 1959 opener on January 7th. On the December 20th edition of the show, Balkin introduced the man who would be the backbone of Evansville wrestling up through the selling of the local office to the Indianapolis Wrestling Club – Rip Hawk.

Hawk would be the featured star for the three weeks without live action at the Coliseum, Balkin building him to headline the January 7th show. The first *Studio Wrestling* of 1959 would be a mix of Nashville and St. Louis wrestlers, with Al Green, who would appear here for Jerry Jarrett in the early to mid-70s, announced to face Chief Suni War Cloud but instead defeating Carlos Rodriguez and Hawk going over Chick Garibaldi, the youngest member of the wrestling clan that had been active in the Evansville promotion since the 30s.

The following Wednesday would see Hawk make his Coliseum debut in the main event against a babyface Dick Beyer. At the time, Beyer was a former Syracuse football standout who had transitioned to coaching as part of the Detroit Lions staff. In the off season, he would wrestle and had previously worked in Evansville in May of 1958 against Tor Yamata. In a few years, when working in Los Angeles, Beyer would adopt the masked persona that would make him a legend… "The Super Intelligent Destroyer." But in 1959, he was a four year veteran wrestling as an All-American football star babyface.

The rest of the season opening card was announced as strongman Adrian Baillargeon making his first visit to the city in five years to meet Chief War Cloud and Chick Garibaldi against Al Green to open. The night would see Hawk, War Cloud and Garibaldi taking the winner's share from their matches.

The following Saturday at Channel 7 would be announced as Garibaldi facing off with a member of another famous wrestling family, Danny Dusek, followed by Rip Hawk against Tommy O'Toole. But what the viewers saw instead was a rematch of the prior week's feature match as Hawk and Garibaldi would clash again, with Chick giving the Hawk his first loss in Evansville. This would be setting up the January 14th event at the Coliseum where they would take the TV rivalry to a paying audience in the main event. Their scheduled TV opponents would also be at the Coliseum on the 14th. O'Toole would defeat Baillargeon 2 falls to 1 and Danny Dusek would defeat Nashville's Jerry Miller in the one-fall opener. As for the main event, it's never a good sign when you see the Athletic Commissioner involved in the results.

Officially, it's recorded that the match was declared a no contest in the third fall – but the finish was much more chaotic than the record book shows. Garibaldi would pick up the first fall in 10:30 and, after the break, Hawk would even things up at the 7:15 mark. In the third fall, it all broke down and, four minutes in, referee Wayne Pate would get knocked down in the melee and Deputy Athletic Commissioner Forest Emery would stop the match, declaring the finish a No Contest draw. Emery would also fine both Hawk and Garibaldi $50 each - $440 apiece in today's money – for roughing up Pate and order a rematch.

There's always a debate on if Athletic Commissioners were smartened up or not. In some territories it's obvious they weren't, while in others their actions indicate they probably were. In the case of Forest Emery, I lean towards him being smart to the business. Having built the Hawk/Garibaldi feud on the *Studio Wrestling* show, Balkin drew what the *Evansville Press* called "a capacity crowd" on the 14th. With the 18th annual March of Dimes benefit card set for the 21st, Emery's order booked a potential sell out. It's not clear if Emery and Balkin had it planned this way, but if we go by the Dick Anderson column in Saturday's *Press*, the turnout on the 14th was a surprise to Leon…

"Wednesday loomed forbiddingly, there was a prediction of rain, and a threat of snow or worse. For Leon Balkin it was old stuff. Wednesday is wrestling night at the Coliseum. Traditionally, it rains, blows or snows on Wednesday night. Or Evansville College plays Butler or Purdue.

For several years now the veteran wrestling promoter has been struggling to keep his hat above the low-water level. Most of the time he's been in up to his ears. While other wrestling centers reported increasing crowds, reawakening of interest, Leon has only the darkest of work sheets to offer for his efforts.

Somehow, some way, he stuck with it. And he even weathered efforts of rival promoters to cut into his territory, force him out or buy him out. He found it difficult to bring to Evansville so-called top men in the mat game because the paychecks were too small. He picked carefully the men he could get.

On Wednesday his advance ticket sale indicated something was happening. He went to the Coliseum with over a $200 advance, as against $13 the week previously. And he hoped the rain would hold off.

And at 8 o'clock, thirty minutes before time for the first bout, the Coliseum lobby was jammed, there were lines all the way outside. As it turned out it was a capacity house, not overflowing, but capacity. And it didn't begin raining until 8:30.

'What happened? I don't know, I wish I knew,' said Leon. 'But whatever it was, I'm happy about it. It was like old times. We've had some of the wrestlers on TV, the main event, Chick Garibaldi and Rip Hawk looked good, but it was something else. I'm

Saturday's TV promised the potential for a replay of the third fall with both Hawk and Garibaldi scheduled to appear. TV listings indicated Chick would be wrestling Danny Dusek, as he was supposed to the previous week, while Rip would be in the ring with Buddy Smith. Nothing out of the ordinary was reported in the articles previewing the benefit card on the 21st. Along with the grudge match between Hawk and Garibaldi, Balkin continued his tradition of booking "special attraction" acts for his charity shows. This time around it would be the midgets Lord Littlebrook and Bull Brummell facing off in the semi-main event. The opener was set to be Danny Dusek and Tommy O'Toole in a 2-out of-3 fall, 45 minute time limit match up.

Unfortunately, Littlebrook and Brummell did not arrive in Evansville. Instead, Tiny Tim would come back after dropping the first fall to defeat Fuzzy Cupid. Dusek and O'Toole would split the first two falls of their match before going to a time limit draw in the third. And the main event saw Rip Hawk come out the winner of the grudge match by taking the 1st and 3rd falls. The victory came at the 6:00 mark as both men collided, bumping heads with Garibaldi getting the worst of it, allowing Hawk to cover him for the pin. A clean pin for the heel, but just fluky enough to keep Garibaldi strong and keep fan interest should the pair be matched up again. Crowd numbers were not released so there's no indication of how blizzard conditions that night affected turnout, but the March of Dimes' cut of the gate would be $194, or a little over $1,800 today.

The *Studio Wrestling* listing for January 24th would give Rip Hawk vs. Bobby Bruns and Tommy O'Toole vs. Billy McDaniel as the featured bouts. No Chick Garibaldi, but he would not be forgotten. The third Hawk/Garibaldi meeting at the Coliseum would be announced, as would be the bout's special referee… former boxing champion Joey Maxim.

Maxim, who in 1959 was the only man to defeat both Floyd Patterson and Sugar Ray Robinson, was retired from the ring and touring the Southern wrestling promotions, sometime serving as a special referee and occasionally working boxer-vs-wrestler matches. He was still enough of a name that Balkin brought him in as an extra draw for this second main event rematch. The card, on the 28th felt very much like a "make-good." A local star of the last few years, Tor Yamata, was being brought in for the single fall opener against Detroit grappler Lou Klein and the midgets were scheduled again, with Tiny Tim tagging with Lord Littlebrook in a 2-out of-3 fall contest against Fuzzy Cupid and Bull Brummel.

Despite the Norte Dame football coach being in town and Evansville College hosting Butler, a big crowd was expected and would see Garibaldi take the first fall, but Hawk win the war by getting pins in Falls 2 & 3 after back body drops on the Italian star. But his tactics would also lead to conflict with the special referee, as Maxim would drop the roughneck from New Mexico twice during the bout. In the other matches, Tiny Tim and Lord Littlebrook would win the midget tag match, while Yamata would pin Klein.

The heat between Hawk and the former light-heavyweight boxing champ would continue on Saturday's *Studio Wrestling* show. The TV listings for January 31st promised a ladies match between "Cuban Bombshell" China Mira and Jessica Rogers as well as Rip Hawk against Bob Bozer. What the folks at home actually got to see was another dust-up between Hawk and the 39-year-old former champ. As a result, Leon Balkin would book the pair in a "boxer-vs-wrestler" bout Wednesday night.

February 1959

Press coverage leading up to the February 4th card would focus on Joey Maxim and the stipulations of the match. Maxim would be wearing 10-ounce gloves while Rip Hawk would be bare-handed and, rather than a time-limit for best of three falls, there would be 8 rounds lasting two minutes each. The night would also feature a ladies 2-of-3 match with China Mira and Jessica Rogers facing off with a 45 minute time limit and a tag match seeing Tor Yamata paired with Wild Bill Longson against Chick Garibaldi and Tommy O'Toole.

On the 4th, Jessica Rogers would win the semi-main when Mira refused to break a choke hold in the third fall, leading to a DQ. The opening tag match would wind up a 1-1 draw as neither duo could get the third fall pin before time expired. As for the main event, it would be a wild affair. The report from the *Evansville Press* claimed a "Standing Room Only" crowd of over 2,500 witnessing Hawk recover from being knocked to the canvas 13 times to eke out a pin in the 6th round. In that round, Hawk took advantage a minute in. After ducking a wild right hook, the villainous grappler caught Maxim in a headlock and rolled him into a reverse crab. Newspaper reports would describe Hawk as being "as unpopular as a baby-snatcher with the local fans," but only a month into 1959 he had managed to revive the fortunes of the Evansville NWA office and Leon Balkin. But after such a hot start to year and both the youngest Garibaldi and a former boxing champ vanquished, the question became would they maintain the momentum.

In February of 1959 the WTVW prime time line-up consisted of Dick Clark's nighttime Rock and Pop variety show, Country and Bluegrass with *Jubilee USA*, the "Champaign Music" of Lawrence Welk and then "*Sammy Kaye's Music From Manhattan.*" Not exactly the perfect lead-in for *Studio Wrestling*, but in those days of only three local channels it worked. Late in the week, Leon Balkin indicated he would look to book Tor Yamata as Rip Hawk's next Coliseum opponent. This Saturday night, TV listings would have Yamata scheduled to meet Tennessee icon Len Rossi and Chick Garibaldi up against French Canadian Adrian Baillargeon. Booking a heel-vs-heel match as the Wednesday feature was a risk, but a calculated one on Balkin's part. Yamata had a fairly successful heel run locally in 1958 and with a number of WW2 veterans and former wartime factory workers in the crowd, it would take an act of God to turn the Japanese star into a babyface. Hawk was the new hot heel act, but with his blonde hair and rugged good looks, there was potential for him to be a babyface draw as well. Something that would be helpful if Balkin were to bring in new NWA champion Pat O'Connor and use Hawk as the challenger.

For the rest of the card February 11th, Balkin would break with his pattern by booking a three-match undercard rather than the usual two matches. Baillargeon would open in a one fall match with Bobby Bruns. Another single fall match would see Jesse James take on Jack McCarthy. The semi-main would feature Chick Garibaldi against a "newcomer" to the area, The Great Bolo.

At this point in time, the Great Bolo was a man by the name of Al Lovelock. Lovelock created the masked persona while splitting time between Hawaii and Los Angeles in 1954. From 1955 to 1958 he would work Dory Funk's Amarillo territory and then move onto the Fields brothers' Gulf Coast promotion. As the Fields were related by marriage to Roy Welch, it's most likely Bolo and McCarthy – who would become Gulf Coast tag champions in 1960 – were booked through the Nashville office... Though why they would leave the Gulf Coast in early February is a mystery. A possibility could be this was in the window between Texas and Florida for Bolo and he was working spots while waiting for an opening in Gulf Coast and did this show as a favor for Balkin. Under his real name, Lovelock appeared in Evansville in 1940 and was a regular for Balkin from 1948 to 1952.

As for the night of the 11th, Bruns and James would win their single-fall matches and the Great Bolo would win the semi-final of the night when the referee stopped the match between the second and third falls due to the condition of Garibaldi following the two headbutts that gave Bolo the second frame. Referee Wayne Pate would also be involved in the stoppage of the main event, but he wouldn't know it.

In the third fall between Hawk and Yamata, Pate would suffer a blow to the head when knocked to the canvas by Yamata, leading Deputy Commissioner Forest Emery to declare the third fall a No Contest and ordering the purse for both wrestlers be held up.

This was the storyline going into Saturday's television where Hawk was listed to face Rocco Spindola out of the

Nashville office and Yamata was scheduled against Herb Welch. A rare third match, between Jessica Rogers and Nora Baker, would also be in the local listings. Hawk and Yamata were both still being booked as heels going into their rematch on the 18th.

That night at the Coliseum, the Gulas/Welch influence on booking was strong. Tommy O'Toole would be booked in the opener against Wild Red Roberts, who also worked as "Rowdy" Red Roberts in Tennessee. The match in the middle would be a tag team affair with local babyfaces Garibaldi and Jesse James taking on "world tag team champions" (Tennessee version), Jackie and Don Fargo. [Technically, the Corsica Brothers were the Gulas/Welch NWA Tag champions at the time, but since the Tennessee TV rarely reached into the Evansville market, the promoters were able to fudge a bit.] To goose the house, Balkin informed the press Tuesday night that two referees would work the Hawk/Yamata main event – One in the ring and the other on the apron. But while this guaranteed a finish, it didn't keep things from getting out of hand.

Hawk would continue his unbeaten streak at the Coliseum, taking the third fall with two standing body drops and a press, he then continued to attack Yamata after the bell rang. If the plan was to turn Hawk babyface, it didn't work as three Evansville Police officers were needed to escort Rip to the dressing room once the post-match fight was broken up. Earlier in the night the Fargo Brothers topped Garibaldi and James while O'Toole won the opener.

With Hawk firmly entrenched as the top bad guy, a new babyface challenger would be needed. Of the Coliseum regulars – Garibaldi, James and O'Toole – Jesse James would get the nod. Saturday morning the 21st he would be announced as Hawk's next opponent as part of a double main event on the 25th. That night's *Studio Wrestling* would need to sell James as a new rival for Hawk, who was scheduled to battle Billy Sharbet. The only other listed match would be Tor Yamata against Jack Dunn. Another match that would need to be built up would be the return of the Fabulous Fargos against Tommy O'Toole with Tex Riley as his partner. The opener would have Hawk's last two foes, Garibaldi and Yamata, facing off.

While he's not remembered as a major star today, James was a solid pick to take on Hawk as Balkin was building to a visit from the NWA Champion. At this time, Jesse was the NWA Southern Junior Heavyweight Champion...The belt that local fans would later see defended regularly as the Jarretts' Southern Heavyweight title. That title wasn't one used by the Evansville office in 1959, but it was an indication of the faith promoters had in him. Pre-match publicity played up the fact that James started training under Jim Londos at the age of 15 and turned pro two years later.

The night of the 25th would open with a 20-minute draw between Yamata and Garibaldi. The Fargos would take the first and third falls of the tag match while Hawk would do the same – in his case needing a combined 2:15 to win the first and third falls while the second fall would see James use an airplane spin to even things up at the 14:30 mark.

Not the greatest showing for the babyface who would try to get back on track Saturday the 28th on TV as he was scheduled to face Adrian Baillargeon in one match with the only other advertised contest for the show being Len Rossi against Ricardo Cortez. It would likely be on this show that the Hawk/James rematch that had been announced on Friday would get the added stipulation of a shot at the NWA Heavyweight Championship on March 11th going to the winner.

March 1959

Pat O'Connor had won the NWA title on January 9th in St. Louis and Evansville promoter Leon Balkin wasted no time in trying to secure dates with the new champion for the Coliseum. The NWA had a lot riding on O'Connor, as the prior titleholder Dick Hutton – while a capable ring technician – was said by many to lack charisma and tended to not draw as well when he made return appearances to a territory. O'Connor was a native of New Zealand who had represented his home country in the 1948 Pan American Games and was a silver medalist in the 1950 British Empire Games. Later that year, he would join the professional ranks, training under Len Levy. His reign would also become a bone of contention between the St. Louis and Chicago promotional offices, as Windy City promoter Fred Kohler initially did not announce the title change and would only offer a fraction of the champ's usual payoff to O'Connor. The champ would eventually wrestle in Chicago and prove to be a solid draw, but in a couple of years the Chicago office would fall into the control of Verne Gagne and Wally Karbo who would split off to form the AWA – the public reason being that they were unable to secure a title match between O'Connor and Gagne. Threats of a congressional investigation into the NWA's monopoly may also have been part of the reason for the split and creation of the "rival" AWA.

But on March 4th, 1959 that series of events was still down the road. On this night, it would be the heel Rip Hawk against the popular Jesse James to see who would meet the NWA champion on the 11th. Hawk had taken the first and third falls from the Jim Londos protege the prior week and this time they would have a full hour to try and win two falls. The undercard would see Tor Yamata facing Tommy O'Toole with a 45 minute time limit and Chick Garibaldi opening things up against Bob Green in a single fall contest. Garibaldi would pick up the victory, topping Green in 11:45. O'Toole would be awarded his match, having won the first fall and Yamata attacking him prior to the bell being rung for the third resulting in the Japanese wrestler being disqualified. And in the Main Event, it would be Rip Hawk continuing his Coliseum win streak. Despite being disqualified in the first fall, the ring villain would recover to pin James with a body press a little over 9 minutes into the second fall and again less than a minute into the third to secure his championship opportunity.

Balkin would start his promotion of the March 11th show in earnest on the following Friday with an article for the *Evansville Press* announcing the full Wednesday card and – possibly trying to protect his lead heel's heat – mentioning that the champ from New Zealand was now an American citizen and making Chicago his home. This build-up would continue on Saturday night's edition of *Studio Wrestling* as Hawk was scheduled to meet Rocky Jones and Jesse James would look to get back on track in Evansville against Jack McCarthy.

The original announcement of the full card indicated that Tommy O'Toole and Chick Garibaldi might team against wrestlers to be announced later, but an article the day before would prove otherwise. Fans would be treated to a rare 4-match card with O'Toole and Garibaldi opening against each other in a 1-fall, 20 minute bout. Jesse James would also have a 1-fall meeting with Tor Yamata. In a special added attraction, Balkin brought in a 2-out of-3 fall ladies match featuring Penny Banner and Princess Tona Tomah.

Before we get to the World title match, let's take a look at the ladies, because as tacky as it may be to say these days, both were well worth looking at.

Banner was a St. Louis native who was discovered by promoter Sam Muchnick in 1954 while she was working as a waitress in a cocktail lounge. Legend has it that the bar's manager told Muchnick his waitress could do 200 sit-ups and the promoter took the bet. When the waitress did the 200 sit-ups, Muchnick started trying to convince her to start wrestling on his circuit. She would adopt the name "Penny Banner" as well as a heel persona in the ring. One might say she looked like Marilyn, but hit like DiMaggio. While working Memphis between 1956 and 1958, she would actually date Elvis a few times – their last time together only a week before he entered the Army. Along with being booked in Evansville, in 1959 she would marry fellow wrestler Johnny Weaver and give birth to her daughter Wendi.

As for the Princess, she was one of the few "Indian wrestlers" in the business to be a legitimate Native American. She was born on the Whitearth Reservation in Minnesota in 1935 and started wrestling on the carnival circuit at the age of 14. Both she and Banner were trained by women's wrestling czar Billy Wolfe, and Tomah would actually be married to Wolfe for a time in the early 50s.

She was also married to midget wrestler Little Beaver as well as another wrestler, Jerry London. She would eventually settle in Arizona, entering law enforcement as her in-ring career wound down, but still keeping a toe in the business locally.

On the day of the 11th, a confident Leon Balkin opened up the Coliseum balcony by putting 1,200 general admission seats on sale at Woods Drug Store which served as the location for advance ticket sales. That evening, the crowd got to see Rip Hawk lose, not only for the first time at the Coliseum, but lose cleanly to the World Champion. In the third fall of the match, Hawk would intentionally hit referee Wayne Pate. But while that had led to match stoppages by the athletic commissioner previously, this time the match would continue. O'Connor would nail Hawk with a hard forearm and smother the blonde bruiser for the deciding pinfall. Afterwards, Hawk would petition the commissioner for a rematch, claiming Pate held him which allowed O'Connor to land the winning blow. The night's other action saw Princess Tomah recover from losing the first fall to defeat Penny Banner thanks to a DQ in the second fall and catching the blonde in a half crab to win the third. Jesse James would get a victory over Yamata while the babyface battle between O'Toole and Garibaldi would go to the time limit.

Hawk's appeal for another shot at Pat O'Connor's belt would be featured Saturday night during the WTVW live show with the announced matches being Hawk against Donald McMannus and Jesse James vs. Mark Starr. The show would also set up the following Wednesday night, as

James would be back in the main event against Hawk. The TV might also have served as the re-introduction of Chick Garibaldi's March 18th opponent, Morris Shapiro... better known as "the Mighty Atlas." Atlas would be a regular for Gulas-Welch around this time, holding most of the Nashville/Birmingham area titles. He would have a run in Evansville in 1958 and was unbeaten with the exception of one match against then-World champion Dick Hutton. The opening match would be announced with Tommy O'Toole, who – thanks to a number of time limit draws – had quietly built up an undefeated singles record at the Coliseum, facing off against former National Wrestling *Association* champion Wild Bill Longson in a 1-fall, one hour time limit match. But that was not to be as Longson would not make it to Evansville that night. Instead O'Toole would face Tor Yamata and wrestle to a draw at the 30 minute mark. Garibaldi would take home a winner's purse in the semi-main event. After splitting the first two falls, referee Ralph Hamilton would disqualify the Mighty Atlas just shy of seven minutes into the third when the strongman would not release a hold before the official completed his count. In the final, Hawk would have to rally but the blonde bomber would manage to improve to 3-0 against James, winning fall #2 following a knee to the cowboy's head and another to the throat. Fall #3's pin coming after a back body drop.

While he was not listed on Saturday's TV page, Hawk's petitioning of the athletic commission for a championship rematch would continue, as would the rebuilding of Chick Garibaldi. He was listed to face Chico Cortez while Tor Yamata was booked with Danny Dusek. If those matches took place, it would have been a long weekend for Garibaldi. The Saturday *Evansville Press*' announcement of Wednesday's card claimed Chick was spending the weekend in St. Louis with brother Ralph in preparation for Wednesday as he would be getting a shot at Hawk for the first time in weeks, with an NWA World Title match at stake. The March 25th Coliseum show would also have Bill Longson announced again, teaming with Adrian Baillargeon against Bobby Bruns and Jesse James. The opening match of Johnny Keane against Rocky Smith would not be revealed until Sunday. Smith would go onto greater fame in the 60s and early 70s as part of the masked Infernos tag team, but in 1959 Evansville he was a talented young newcomer who gave Rip Hawk all he could handle during a recent edition of *Studio Wrestling*.

On Wednesday, Hawk would be in his heel glory. His appeals to promoter Balkin and deputy athletic commissioner Forest Emery to grant him a championship rematch due to the actions of referee Pate had been ignored. Instead, to get another shot at Pat O'Connor, he would have to overcome not just one man...but three! His scheduled opponent – Chick Garibaldi, referee Wayne Pate – who he blamed for his lone Coliseum loss, and now Ralph Garibaldi, who had headlined Evansville in the past and would be in brother Chick's corner.

Hawk would once again be a slow starter, dropping the initial fall to the young Italian, but would rally savagely in the second – taking the match out to the floor and battering young Garibaldi before returning to ring. Between falls, referee Pate determined Garibaldi would not be able to continue and awarded the match and championship opportunity to Hawk. As for the other matches, the babyface team of Bruns and James would rally and defeat Longson and Baillargeon two falls to one while Keane and Smith would go to a time limit draw.

Rip Hawk's dominance in the Evansville ring had now gone on for almost three months without any real local threat, but that would change with the March 28th television.

One of the foundations of professional wrestling that formed as the sport shifted from shoot fights to worked exhibitions was the battle between good and evil. White hat vs. Black hat, good guys and bad guys, heel vs. face, no matter how you want to describe it this basic conflict is what has drawn people to the arenas or glued their eyes to the television set. If you have a lead heel and a lead babyface who both have a charisma that registers with the audience you're going to have a goldmine at the box office and history bears this out. The greatest year for the Memphis promotion was 1982 when the Jerry Lawler/Jimmy Hart feud hit its peak and the Fabulous Ones were battling Hart's tag teams. One could argue the peak for the AWA was Hulk Hogan's chase for Nick Bockwinkel's world title. The only time WCW wasn't a money pit on the Turner Broadcasting ledger was the arrival of the nWo as the "big bad" for the WCW roster to rally around and fight off. In March of 1959, Leon Balkin had his charismatic heel in Rip Hawk, but you could argue the babyface side was severely lacking.

Since the start of the year, Balkin had been using three babyfaces on a regular basis – Chick Garibaldi, Jesse James and Tommy O'Toole. Garibaldi and James were now 0-3 against Hawk in the 2-out of-3 fall matches. O'Toole had yet to face Hawk at the Coliseum, but he also had yet to really break out with his "undefeated record" filled with 20 and 30 minute time limit draws. With Pat O'Connor not available for the first April card, a new good guy was needed and on Saturday night the 28th, he would debut.

The March 28th *Studio Wrestling* listing did not show the familiar names for the week's announced matches. Tennessee regular Tex Riley was scheduled to face Joe Millich while Joe McCarthy would return to Evansville to face a newcomer – Farmer Don Marlin.

There's not a lot of information out there about Don Marlin. His earliest listed pro matches are from Hawaii in 1944 and 1945. Nothing is listed for 1946, but in 1947 he would make two appearances in Evansville booked through the "Mississippi Valley Sports Club," and then nothing until 1949 where he turns up in the Chicago area having adopted the "Farmer Marlin" gimmick, wrestling in work boots or barefoot and wearing blue jeans held up by a rope belt instead of tights. As he would be billed as being from Angola, IN, the persona would be slightly more refined than the hillbilly gimmick, but still play off the hillbilly fad of the late 1950s. He also had the distinction of having helped to draw what was then the largest gate for wrestling at the International Ampitheatre in Chicago when he faced Gorgeous George. In later years, there would be some confusion locally with Evansville Police Lt. Gene Martin who entered the business about this time being said to have wrestled as "Farmer Martin." This was probably due to Marlin and Martin serving as co-promoters locally in 1962 and the local papers' tendency to misspell wrestler names.

Farmer Marlin's TV appearance (and an unlisted one by Bobby Bruns who had gotten the rub by teaming with Jesse James the prior Wednesday) was likely what set up the unusual main event that would take place on the April 1st Coliseum show.

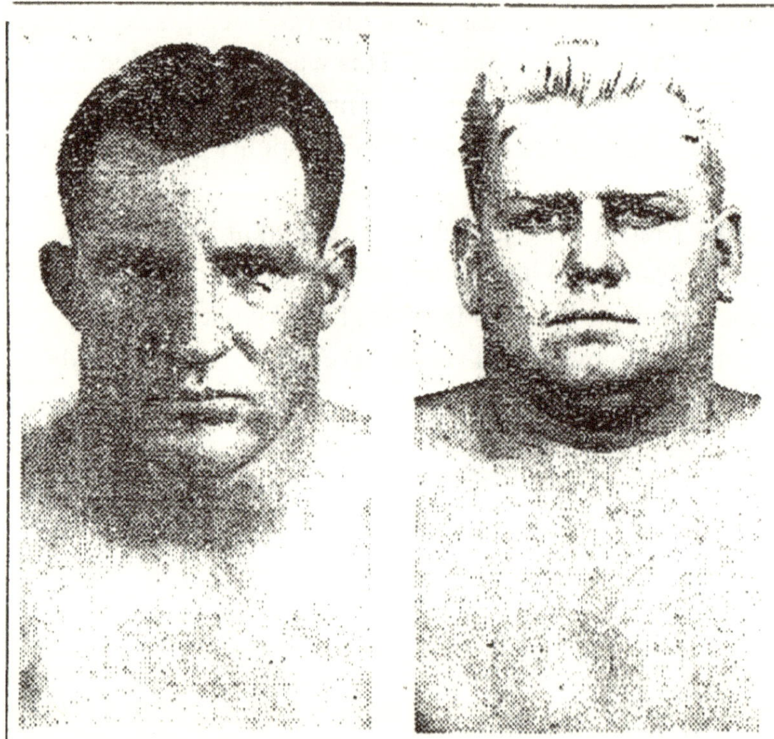

Promotional blurb from the March 10, 1959 *Evansville Press*

April 1959

On Sunday, March 29th, those who did not tune into *Studio Wrestling* learned via the *Courier & Press* that Rip Hawk had agreed to take on two men Wednesday. The Hawk would meet both Bobby Bruns and Farmer Marlin one-on-one and forfeit his pay for the night if he could not defeat both men within an hour's time. The order of the matches would be decided by coin toss. Other matches would have Chick Garibaldi scheduled against Wild Bill Longson and a 20 minute opener to feature Chico Cortez. On that April's Fools Day night, Cortez would be dispatched by Billy Scharbet in 8 minutes; Garibaldi and Longson would go to the 45 minute time limit tied at a fall apiece and Bobby Bruns would win the coin toss but fall to Hawk after 10 minutes. To win the villain's money, Farmer Marlin would have to last 50 minutes, but would wind up getting the win 45 seconds after the bell rang. As he jumped into the ring before Hawk had risen from pinning Bruns, Marlin would nail Hawk in the head with his work boot, knocking the heel out cold. While the crowd celebrated the blonde bully's comeuppance, Deputy Commissioner Emery would rain on the parade, ordering a rematch between Hawk and Marlin because the Farmer was not wearing regulation wrestling shoes. The rematch would also be a regulation match, 2 out of 3 falls.

Along with the Hawk/Marlin rematch, Friday's newspapers would also announce Bruns teaming with Tommy O'Toole against Bill Longson and Billy McDaniel while Chick Garibaldi would be in the one fall opener.

Hawk and Marlin would be the featured stars in the *Studio Wrestling* listings, with Hawk scheduled to face Chief Red Cloud (whose name was misspelled as "Red Clown" by the typesetter) and the Farmer up against Charlie Keane. It would be on this TV the rematch would get an added stipulation of Hawk's April 15th shot at Pat O'Connor being on the line. It would also be revealed that Garibaldi's Wednesday opponent would be Joe McCarthy and, somewhere along the line, Billy McDaniel would be replaced in the tag bout by Tor Yamata due to the former suffering a knee injury in St. Louis Friday.

It's also possible NWA champion Pat O'Connor was in the WTVW Carpenter House studios that night, as Tuesday's *Evansville Press* featured a photo of O'Connor signing the contract for the 15th flanked by Leon Balkin, Marlin, and Hawk, who was in his trunks and ring jacket. The show would end with fans at home thinking Hawk's championship dreams would end Wednesday, as the heel would again be knocked out cold by Marlin during the program.

On April 8th, Chick Garibaldi would defeat Charlie Keane at 15:20 after hitting the Birmingham native with three bulldozer shoulder blocks and a body press. The team of Bruns and O'Toole would escape with a victory after Yamata and Longson were disqualified. And in the main event, Hawk would get his revenge, but it wouldn't come easily. With the memory of the blonde bomber being knocked out on live TV fresh in everyone's mind, Hawk would be the aggressor – winning the first fall in 10:20 after catching the Farmer in an atomic bomb...based on descriptions, this was similar to the "bombs away" move used by Matt Borne in the 80s and renamed the "whoopie cushion" when Borne worked as Doink the Clown in the 90s, only with the wrestler landing on his opponent with his knees rather than his rump. Another atomic bomb attempt in the second fall would miss, giving Marlin an opening and after working on Hawk's "injured" knee, the Farmer picked up the fall at the 4:00 mark. It would all break down in the third fall, with Rip getting the win 3:15 in after he rammed Marlin's head into the ringpost.

On Friday afternoon, Balkin would release the scheduled card for the 15th of April, with the O'Connor/Hawk championship tilt as the headliner. Don Marlin would be back on Wednesday in the semi-main, taking on Tor Yamata. And with the champ in town, there would be four matches on the card rather than the usual three. One fall contests would see Chick Garibaldi and Bobby Bruns facing off while Tommy O'Toole would be paired against Bill Longson. Saturday's *Studio Wrestling* show would see Hawk and Marlin in the listed matches – Marlin facing Chico Cortez and Hawk getting Eddie Davis for his opponent.

Saturday's TV would be the kickoff of a promotional blitz on the part of the local NWA office. The first meeting between O'Connor and Hawk drew well, but now it was mid-April and weather was improving to where the threat of a freak snowstorm would not be as likely to keep fans away. Sunday's *Courier & Press* would not only have the usual preview of Wednesday's event, but the weekly column by Steve Perkins would be a profile of Rip Hawk.

There, local fans would learn the bad man from New Mexico was really 28-year old Rip Perna from Alburquerque (which was fiction) who was married to a brunette named Eleanor, his father had been a minor league baseball player and he paid his taxes on the estimated $15,000 to $20,000 he made as a main event worker. Oh, and he packed a .32 pistol in his wrestling bag.

Tuesday's preview in the *Evansville Press* would also help set up the follow-up card on the 22nd, with a mention that Farmer Marlin offered to put up $500 to get a rematch with Hawk no matter how the title match turned out. But the focus remained on the night of the 15th. In the opener, Bobby Bruns would top fellow babyface Garibaldi, O'Toole and Longson would go to a time limit draw and Farmer Marlin would withstand the judo mastery of Tor Yamata to win the semi-final 2 falls to 1. Then it was time for the bout the near-capacity crowd came to see.

Newspaper reports describe the audience being "in an uproar throughout" the one hour time limit match. Hawk would finally take the first fall at the 36:10 mark, catching the champ with a back body drop and following up with a body press. After the short break, O'Connor would capture the second fall 11:20 into the action via a rolling cradle into a pin. The third fall would be a stalemate with neither man gaining the advantage before time expired, allowing the NWA kingpin to retain the title.

The following Friday morning, the *Evansville Courier* would have the announcement that Hawk had accepted Marlin's challenge and the next Wednesday night's main event would be "winner takes all" with no time limit – the latter stipulation likely due to feeling the time limit cost him the NWA title much as the referee had in March. No other matches were announced, but the supporting card would reportedly include Jesse James, Bobby Bruns, Tommy O'Toole and newcomer Otto Von Krupp of Germany, who would debut in town on Saturday night.

The listing for *Studio Wrestling* promised a ladies match with Nell Stewart vs. Laura Martinez and a tag bout with Bruns and O'Toole meeting the team of Otto Von Krupp and Rip Hawk.

It would be on this show that the full card would be unveiled with Von Krupp in the semi-final spot against Tommy O'Toole and Bobby Bruns facing Red McIntyre. By Wednesday, however, there would be changes to the opening match. Bruns and McIntyre would be out and Chick Garibaldi would be back to meet Chico Cortez with a special added match of Tor Yamata against Tito Romero.

The night of the 22nd would see Garibaldi capture the opener in 10:30 with an abdominal stretch and Yamata's judo chops leveling Romero at 16:10. In the semi-main event, Tommy O'Toole's Irish luck finally ran out. After winning the first fall, O'Toole would struggle and drop the next two falls to Von Krupp in a combined 2:40. It would be an ever rougher night for Farmer Marlin. 27 minutes into the main event, he would pin Hawk after three mule kicks and a body press, but the second fall would go out onto the floor and as the Farmer tried to reenter the ring, Hawk would nail Marlin with a flying tackle sending the babyface to the floor with a thud. 20 seconds later, the second fall was awarded to the Hawk and after the break he would be named winner of the match and the $500 when Marlin was unable to answer the bell for the third fall.

The New Mexico roughneck would be scheduled against Buddy Hackett for *Studio Wrestling* Saturday with Joe Millich and Chris Belkas facing off in the other listed match for the 25th of April, but one suspects much more happened to set up the next Wednesday night. Hawk would be taking on his tag partner from the prior week's television... Otto Von Krupp. And like the match with Farmer Marlin, there would be no time limit.

Now, the name Otto Von Krupp may not register with fans who got into wrestling after 1960, but that name and persona was used by Larry Simon prior to his adopting the "Boris Malenko" identity he would use to the end of his career. If the Evansville Von Krupp was in fact Simon, then this would be one of the first areas he used the gimmick that he would take to the AWA in 1961 prior to becoming The Great Malenko in Florida.

Also on the 29th, Bruns and O'Toole would meet Eric Von Brock and Tor Yamata in an Australian Rules tag team match and Farmer Marlin would start his climb back up the ladder against Chris Belkas. That night would see the opening match stopped after Belkas injured his shoulder and the heel team of Yamata and Von Brock would dispatch Bruns and O'Toole 2 falls to 1. In the heel-on-heel main event, Von Krupp would take the first fall, getting Hawk to submit to what the newspapers described as "a reverse inverted bear hug" at the 5:55 mark. But falls two and three would be more brawling than mat wrestling, with

Hawk picking up both falls by repeatedly smashing the German's head into the ring post.

Four months into 1959 and the NWA's Evansville office had new life thanks to the arrival of Rip Hawk, not to mention the popularity of the live Saturday night TV show on the city's only VHF signal. It was so popular that even in the colder weather months of March and April, fans were lining up to be part of the studio audience... Which led to this letter to the editor in the April 21st *Evansville Press*...

WHY?

To the Editor of The Press:
In regard to the WTVW studio wrestling on Saturday nights, I would like for Mr. Leon Balkin to answer one question. Why is it that some people are allowed to go in to the studio at the front door while the majority have to stand on the outside at the side enterance an hour or so before the open up the side entrance? Are they any better than anybody else?
There is one lady, 79 years old, who has to stand outside and if she can, then why can't the others? We may be free loaders on Saturday nights, but not on Wednesday nights.
We also would like to see Rip Hawk and Otto Vankrupp wrestle together. – B.F.W.

The "freeloader" line came from comments that Rip Hawk had made in a recent radio interview and he no doubt tossed the line around during the TV show to taunt the crowd. 24 hours later, readers of the Press would see a response from none other than promoter Balkin...

Mr. Balkin Answers

To the Editor of The Press:
This is an answer to B.F.W.
Dear B.F.W.
I would like to state at this time that I have nothing to do with the admittance of people who come to WTVW studio to witness the Saturday night wrestling bouts. First of all you have to write to WTVW channel 7 for tickets, and another thing they have a special door on the side to gain entrance to the studio. This is not a question of free loaders. WTVW has the right to invite people to watch their live wrestling shows on Saturday nights. The side entrance is for employes(sic), and other personnel connected with WTVW and we do not beg anyone to attend our weekly Wednesday night bouts, if they don't want to. But I do want to say that I don't have anything to do with the admittance of the fans on Saturday night. All I do is act as matchmaker for WTVW Channel 7.
Trusting that I have answered you to the best of my knowledge.
-Leon Balkin

Capacity crowds at the Coliseum. Turning them away at the TV studio. Leon Balkin had one more building to conquer in Evansville, and just before the show on the 29th, he received the means to do so. Pat O'Connor's date for May

13th in Jackson, Mississippi was canceled and awarded to Evansville.

CHAMP SIGNS FOR COLISEUM BOUT—World wrestling champion Pat O'Connor is shown signing for the title match to be held April 15 at the Coliseum. Looking on are (left to right) Rip Hawk, Promoter Leon Balkin and Farmer Marlin. Hawk and Marlin will grapple Wednesday night to see who will meet O'Connor in the championship match.

Promotional photo from April 7, 1959 *Evansville Press*

PHOTO COLLAGE FROM THE MAY 12, 1959 EVANSVILLE PRESS FOR THE BALKIN/MUCHNICK CO-PROMOTED STADIUM SHOW.

May 1959

On May 1st, Balkin revealed plans for perhaps his most ambitious show so far this year. After being awarded NWA Champion Pat O'Connor's May 13th date when a card in Jackson, Mississppi on that date fell through, Leon would book that date at Roberts Municipal Stadium for the third meeting between O'Connor and local sensation Rip Hawk. The same building he swore he'd never use again after a poor turnout in 1957.

Balkin partnered with the office of St. Louis promoter and NWA President Sam Muchnick for this event which would feed off of the time limit draw in April's rematch between Hawk and O'Connor. Their first meeting would also figure into the Stadium show as Balkin announced he was seeking a new referee as part of Hawk's demands if he were to sign the contract because of local ref Wayne Pate's actions costing him the title back in March. Balkin and Muchnick promised a packed card with a dozen stars scheduled to appear at the show benefiting the *Evansville Press*' Youth Fund – the charity being promised 25% of the gross gate receipts after taxes.

The show was especially ambitious, seeing as how Balkin had less than two weeks to promote it. He was averaging well over 2,000 fans every Wednesday at the Coliseum, but the two and a half-year old Stadium held six times that. He needed to make the 13th of May a special day, but before then he had two TV shows and a Wednesday night card to book.

Studio Wrestling on May 2nd was be the first step. For the first time in a while, Rip Hawk would not be seen in the newspaper listing for the TV show. This week, the listings promised Steve Belkas vs. Mark Starr and Chief Red Cloud against Eric Von Brock. Von Brock was a rookie who would go onto fame working under the name Rock Hunter, eventually becoming a manager in the early days of cable wrestling on WTBS. He also achieved a bit of infamy in the early 80s, getting more or less blackballed after participating in newspaper expose on the business.

The other spotlighted star in the listing was Steve Belkas, who was far from being a rookie. Belkas broke in around 1931 and primarily worked under the name "Marco Polo" and also used the ring names "Steve Karas" and "Ted Bell." It's possible he was working in the Central States territory as the kayfabe brother of Chris Belkas who had been "injured" on the March 29th Coliseum card. (Chris Belkas, by the way, was for a time the father-in-law of Superstar Billy Graham.)

Either way, the Saturday night TV had to build up two shows. Both the big event for May 13th as well as the regular Coliseum card on May 6th. It's very possible that the show revealed an alliance between Von Brock and Rip Hawk's last opponent, Otto Von Krupp, who would in a few years go on to become "The Great Malenko."

We say the alliance may have been shown on TV, because the Coliseum main event this week would be the Germans facing Farmer Marlin and Tommy O'Toole. Other matches would have Tor Yamata scheduled to face Steve Belkas and Chick Garibaldi vs. Chief Red Cloud in the opener.

That Red Cloud/Garibaldi match wound up not happening instead Len Rossi would dispatch Rocky Smith with a dropkick at 13:30 into a 30 minute time limit. Yamata and Steve Belkas were tied at a fall apiece when their 45 minute time limit expired. And in the main event, the Farmer and the Irishman would be declared the winners, but came out the worse for wear. Referee Pate disqualified the German team in the third fall for repeatedly jumping on Marlin's leg which they had draped across the ropes.

Thursday had the announcement of more matches on the stadium card – Specifically the women's match. Lorraine Johnson, who was half of the Women's tag team champions with Penny Banner, was announced to face Kay Noble of Missouri, who was being billed as a future champion. She'd never win the Women's World title thanks to the stranglehold the Fabulous Moolah had on the belt, but she had won the regional women's championships in the Amarillo and Central States territories and the AWA women's title in 1963. A few months before the stadium show, Noble and Johnson – along with Penny Banner and Laura Martinez – were actually charged by police with inciting a riot at a show where the four women began fighting outside the ring. They plead "not guilty" and the promoter paid the fine.

Saturday, May 9th saw the promotion of the Stadium show really kick in. After being off the prior week, Rip Hawk would return to *Studio Wrestling* on WTVW and this event was plugged in Dick Anderson's column in the *Evansville Press*. Anderson would also reveal that 4400 seats would be available at $1 apiece. These were most likely the rickety wooden bleachers that ringed the stadium prior to its late 1980s renovation. Another article in the same edition of the newspaper revealed the remainder of the card, including the midget tag match with Lord Littlebrook and Cowboy Bradley facing Bull Brummel and Tiny Roe. Local stars would also be used with Von Brock in the opener against Steve Belkas and Von Krupp going up against Tommy O'Toole. The *Press* also featured an editorial cartoon promoting the card. Along with the $1 bleacher seats, Ringside and the chairback seats in sections D and M would cost $2.50 each, a full dime higher than the usual Coliseum ringside tickets. All other chairback seats would be $2.

The *Evansville Press*, whose charity stood to benefit from the Stadium card, continued to plug the show beyond Saturday's coverage. The *Sunday Courier and Press* featured a cheesecake shot of Lorraine Johnson that would make Jayne Mansfield jealous. Monday would see a feature article on "Tiny" Howard – the 6'4", 280-pound former wrestler who was tapped to be the special referee for Hawk/O'Connor III. Tuesday's edition featured a massive photo collage of the night's participants and an article heralding the dignitaries coming to Evansville for the show, including Stan Goldberg, president of the State Athletic Commission, promoters Jim Barnett of Indianapolis, Nick Gulas and Roy Welch of Nashville, Wee Willie Davis of Louisville and first NWA champion turned promoter Orville Brown. Wednesday would continue the hard sell with an article promoting a number of seats still available.

The hype helped, no doubt, but visually in a 12,000 seat arena, the crowd had to be disappointing. Approximately 4,000 paid to see O'Connor retain the NWA crown. Rather than give you the results, let's leave it to the words of a young sports reporter who would one day become editor of the Evansville daily newspaper... Tom Tuley.

"The fabulous Rip Hawk, or the 'chicken Hawk' as some of his enemies call him, needs a strong pair of suspenders to hold those pants of his up today because he hasn't got that new belt around his waist after all.

While nearly 4000 people filled spacious Roberts Municipal Stadium with jeers and cat-calls last night, the blond meanie from New Mexico lost to world's heavyweight wrestling champion Pat O'Connor once again, and just when Hawk seemed to have the match in the bag.

The benefit program netted The Press Youth Fund a handsome $1088, one of the most successful in history.

O'Connor, much the faster of the two wrestlers, got off to a good start winning the first fall with an airplane spin. However, Hawk came back strong in the second round, and after softening O'Connor up with a looping haymaker to the jaw, he put the champion out with a pin in six minutes, 45 seconds.

It was then that Hawk paraded about the ring, much to the displeasure of the howling fans, showing how he would look in the world's heavyweight championship wrestling belt.

He seemed ready to take the belt in the third fall, too, as he knocked O'Connor groggy and then prepared to deliver an atom bomb from the top rope. But he missed, and instead bombed referee Joe 'Tiny' Howard.

Howard, the biggest man in the ring, then got up off the mat and disqualified Hawk, who was working O'Connor over in one corner of the ring. Time of the final fall was 1:10.

Although the Hawk-O'Connor fracas was the feature of the night, the hit with the crowd was obviously the midget tag-team match.

Lord Clayton Littlebrook and Cowboy Bradley defeated Bull Brummell and Tiny Roe in the match between the little men, but not before the four had engaged in a free-for-all outside the ring and Referee Wayne Pate had been bitten by Littlebrook.

The team of Brummell and Roe won the first fall in 10 minutes when Cowboy Bradley was carried from the ring with an injured leg. However, the Cowboy came back to win the second fall in 7:10 by flattening Brummell with a reverse off the ropes.

Was 4,000 the maximum for the Evansville area's wrestling audience? Did some Coliseum regulars just not want to go all the way out to the Stadium, then considered to be at the outskirts of town? Had the Hawk/O'Connor rivalry run out of steam?

On the positive side, this was the largest audience for a wrestling card in Evansville in years and the Youth Fund would get over $1,000 from the gate receipts. Also, Leon Balkin would be getting a second consecutive date with the NWA Champion for the Coliseum against a former title holder.

On Saturday, the Sports pages announced Pat O'Connor's return on May 20th against the man he defeated for the NWA strap, Dick Hutton. Rip Hawk would also return to Court Street, working the semi-main against Jesse James. Saturday night's TV revealed the rest of the four-match card with Tommy O'Toole facing Eric Von Brock and Wild Bill Longson against Pat Fraley. Announced matches for *Studio Wrestling* had O'Toole vs. Chief Red Cloud and Hawk looking to get back on track against a returning Chris Belkas.

Much would be made of the "Blonde Bomber" not being in the main event during the run up to the May 20th card, giving local fans one more thing to use as ammunition in their insults for the ring villain. Articles also played up that Hutton had not been defeated in Evansville in five years, dating back to before he defeated Lou Thesz for the World's Championship.

On the night of the 20th, Longson defeated Fraley at 4:24 into the opener with a flying scissors, while Von Brock and O'Toole would go to a time limit draw. The Hawk was victorious when Jesse James was sent to the floor in the third fall and could not answer the 20 count to get back in the ring. In the main event, it looked like Hutton's win streak here would continue and he regained the NWA championship, but referee Wayne Pate – after counting three – ruled that O'Connor's leg was through the ropes, voiding the pin. Hutton would vigorously argue his case that he won, but too vigorously for the tastes of deputy athletic commissioner Forest Emery who disqualified the former champion and declared O'Connor the winner and still champ.

Hutton would stick around Evansville. He was scheduled to appear on the March 23rd *Studio Wrestling* to face Tommy O'Toole while Rip Hawk was booked to meet Carlos Romero. That night, Hutton's rematch with O'Connor was announced for the Coliseum on the 27th. That match being in the main event spot meant Hawk would be relegated to the semi-main once again. This time he'd team with Von Brock against James and Farmer Marlin. The ladies were returning as well with Laura Martinez against Kay Nobel, whom she had trained to enter the business. Farmer Marlin would open by himself against Von Brock.

On the 27th, there would be some changes. Farmer Marlin was replaced in the opener by Emile Dupree, who would defeat Von Brock, and Laura Martinez missed the show, so Princess Tona Tomah filled in – topping Kay Noble. Farmer Marlin was in the building later, teaming with Jesse James as scheduled against Hawk and Von Brock. The babyfaces would win this night, getting the lone pinfall on the German before time expired. In the main event, Hutton took the first fall, but hit his head on the mat in fall #2, leading to an O'Connor pin and victory when Hutton could not continue for the third and deciding fall.

After three weeks with the NWA World's Heavyweight Champion in town, the question for fans had to be, "How can Balkin top this for the month of June?" The answer would come on Friday. That's when the local office announced the return of Gorgeous George to Evansville. Fans would also learn the Hawk and Von Brock team were

going to face Marlin and O'Toole and Wild Bill Longson
would open against an opponent to be announced during
the May 30th edition of *Studio Wrestling*. Unfortunately, we
don't have any announced matches for that show, as this
was the point that the *Press* regularly listing the week's
matches on the Saturday TV page became hit and miss.

June 1959

Before the month of May ended, the public learned Leon Balkin's follow up to three weeks of NWA Champion Pat O'Connor in the main event would be the return to Evansville of the man credited with Milton Berle to have helped sell TV's in the mid-50s, the Human Orchid himself – Gorgeous George.

George had last appeared in Evansville in 1958 during the business' "down" period. Fitting as George was in a bit of a down period himself.

In 1959, George Wagner was 44-years old and 10-years removed from when his star power was enough to get pro wrestling back into Madison Square Garden for the first time in over a decade. After earning over $100,000 a year at his peak, by 1959 he was in need of cash so badly he agreed to drop a hair match in Toronto for the payday. By the time he arrived in Evansville with his valet Cherrie, his hair had grown back to a crew cut, but he continued to wear a wig replicating his famous curly locks to the ring and during interviews.

On June 3rd, the Gorgeous One would be in the main event against Jesse James, and it would be noted by the press that Rip Hawk was in the semi-main for a third straight week. This time he'd be teaming again with Eric Von Brock against Farmer Marlin and Tommy O'Toole. Bill Longson would also be back to open the card against Sammy Ford.

On that Wednesday night, Longson's flying scissors took care of Ford in 16:50. The tag match would give the fans their money's worth, with the heels taking fall number one in 10:25 after O'Toole fell victim to Hawk's "atom bomb" move. Farmer Marlin evened things up at 11:30 of the second fall when he mule kicked the German. Marlin was then be pinned by The Hawk at 4:30 into the deciding fall.

It's good that the opener and semi-final ate a lot of time, even with a slightly later 8:45pm bell time, because if the local fans blinked, they might have missed the main event. James took the opening fall quickly, catching Wagner in a reverse crab only 15 seconds into the bout. Then, the Tennessee cowboy would be awarded the second fall when Gorgeous George refused the referee's order to break a hold.

Friday, June 5th, would see promoter Balkin announce the Wednesday card early with an intriguing main event. Gorgeous George would return, but this time against Rip Hawk. Whether this was an attempt to turn Rip babyface or concern that the June 3rd main event could have killed the box office run the local office had seen, the trigger had been pulled on a rare heel-vs-heel headling match with the rest of the card made up of midgets and ladies. Lord Littlebrook and Bull Brummell would meet in a one fall opener and then come back for a mixed tag match – Littlebrook teaming with Kay Nobel and Brummell paired with Kathy Starr. Saturday night, Hawk and George were set to be the focus of live *Studio Wrestling* show. Rip Hawk in the first match against George Medina with Gorgeous George scheduled to meet Chris Belkas in the second TV contest, but that did not take place as Wagner was a no-show. During the broadcast, the card would probably have been clarified to reveal the ladies would have their own one-on-one single fall match prior to the mixed tag match. But the big news about Wednesday night came on Tuesday.

Tuesday afternoon, a piece on the unique mixed tag match would reveal the main event had been changed from Hawk vs Gorgeous George to a return tag battle between Hawk and Von Brock against Marlin and O'Toole. The reason given for Wagner's canceling the TV appearance Saturday and the Wednesday match being a back injury.

That Wednesday night, Lord Littlebrook would get the nod in the opener, pinning Brummell at 9:03 after a pair of dropkicks and body press. The ladies' single match went to the 20 minute time limit, but the women wound up deciding the mixed tag match as Noble pinned Starr.

In the main event, Farmer Marlin and O'Toole would be awarded the win. In the first fall, Von Brock pinned the Farmer, while O'Toole evened things up in the second by pinning Rip Hawk. But, as they went to the break between falls, things got interesting. After Hawk was pinned, for reasons unexplained, Von Brock refused to leave the ring and go back to the dressing room for the break. Because he wouldn't leave the ring, referee Wayne Pate awarded the third fall to Marlin and O'Toole giving Hawk only his 4th loss at the Coliseum, the other coming in NWA title matches and the 2-on-1 match where Marlin kicked him in the head with his work boots.

So, Balkin had a couple of ways to go for the next week. After 6 months and with a solid record of wins and time limit draws, they could finally pull the trigger on an

O'Toole/Hawk program or they could try again to turn Hawk babyface by have him get into a grudge match with the German Von Brock.

On Friday, the announcement came that O'Toole would get the main event spot against the Blonde Bomber – the match being demanded by Hawk after the Irishman opened a cut over his eye in the tag match. It also came out that the Fabulous Fargos would be returning to Evansville, with Jackie and Don set to meet Farmer Marlin and Len Rossi. Friday's newspapers also promised Chief Red Cloud on Wednesday's card along with Bob Corby, Gino Angelo and Johnny Weaver – but no indication of what they'd be doing until Saturday night.

The *Studio Wrestling* listing for June 13th was a rare case of three matches promised with an even more rare 6-man tag bout. Rip Hawk would align himself with Don Fargo and Sammy Stein against Tommy O'Toole, Farmer Marlin and Len Rossi in the feature. Stein and O'Toole would also meet in singles action as would Fargo and Marlin.

As of Sunday morning, the card was set with Hawk/O'Toole, the Fargos against Marlin and Rossi and a whole new opener of L.A's "Crybaby" Bob Corby against Indian Joe. By Tuesday, Indian Joe was replaced by Chief Red Cloud. In the end, it didn't matter as the opener would go to a 20 minute time limit draw. The Fargos, who were being promoted as the #2 tag team in the nation, were victorious against the team of Marlin and Rossi while the main event was declared a double count-out in the third fall when both men were knocked out after butting heads.

The chaos of the main event's third fall was enough for Balkin to tease trying to book a rematch in Friday's newspapers when he announced a mixed tag return bout with Lord Littlebrook and Kay Nobel against Bull Brummell and Kay Starr. Crybaby Corby would also be announced in the opener against Farmer Marlin. The Saturday TV also continued building to a rematch between Hawk and O'Toole on Wednesday with the featured TV matches announced as O'Toole vs Bill Longson and Hawk against Len Rossi.

On Wednesday, June 24th, it would be a "Double Main Event" night with the Hawk/O'Toole rematch secured for a 2-out of-3 fall with no time limit grudge match along with the mixed tag contest, now set for 2-of-3 and an hour time limit. The opener was changed, with Bob Corby out and Chief Red Cloud plugged in. But there would be a bigger change come bell time. Farmer Marlin won against the Chief by DQ, but the middle match that had been the focus of publicity was completely out the window with all four combatants replaced. It was still a mixed tag, with Cowboy Bradley and Laura Martinez defeating Tiny Roe and Jessica Rogers.

Perhaps to make up for the massive change in the semi-main event, Hawk and O'Toole would go beyond what they did the prior week, upping the ante from a double countout to this match's third fall descending into enough of an out of control brawl that both Farmer Marlin and Chief Red Cloud got involved and referee Wayne Pate had no recourse but to stop the match and declare it a "no contest."

Bob Corby was still in the area, scheduled to appear on the next *Studio Wrestling* against Rip Hawk while Chief Red Cloud would be facing Joe Millich. Also on Saturday night, the stipulation for Hawk and O'Toole's third meeting would be revealed.

For the first time in 1959, Evansville's Coliseum would host a Texas Death Match.

July 1959

We're up to Summer and the heat wasn't just in the wrestling ring. June ended with extreme heat being blamed for 15 deaths in the Eastern and Southern US as well as drought conditions for much of the country. For much of the time the Coliseum hosted professional wrestling, the building lacked air conditioning leading local promoters to either find another site with air conditioning, cut the schedule back to once a month or, in most cases, take the Summer off. But with the box office as hot as the asphalt on Court Street separating the Coliseum from the Courthouse, the local NWA office continued to schedule the Wednesday night cards, moving the opening bell-time to 8:45pm as a concession to the warm weather.

Granted, things were still pretty hot in the ring as well. The month of June ended with two of the year's most successful wrestlers – Rip Hawk and Tommy O'Toole – finally paired up in the main events and their third one-on-one clash would take place on July 1st under Texas Death Match rules.

"Action should be wide open tonight at the Coliseum when Rip Hawk and Tommy O'Toole meet in a Texas Death Match, a form of wrestling in which anything goes.

In the death match falls do not count. There is no time limit, no holds are barred and the disqualification rule is waived. The only way for a wrestler to win is for

The rest of the card would feature the Fabulous Fargo Brothers, Jackie and Don, facing Jesse James and Steve Belkas and a one-fall opener with the returning Tor Yamata against Bob Corby. They would go the full 20 minutes to start the night off while the Fargos would take 2 of the three falls in the tag team semi-final which saw Belkas replaced by Charlie Kean.

As for the main event, O'Toole would start strong, winning the first five falls, but he would be busted open against the ringpost in the sixth fall and not be able to answer the bell to start the 7th , giving Hawk – who had recently moved with his family to Evansville – the victory.

On the following Friday, the next Coliseum main event would be announced and for the first time since the card before May's Stadium show, Rip Hawk would not be scheduled to wrestle. Instead, the Fargos would headline on July 8th against Jesse James and Mike Clancy. The semi-main would see a rematch announced for Tor Yamata and Bob Corby, this time 2-out of-3 falls and a 45 minute time limit. Chief Red Cloud would be announced for the opener, but his opponent was still to be determined.

 The July 4th edition of live *Studio Wrestling* no doubt had fireworks of its own with both Fargos scheduled to appear – Jackie taking on Bob Carlisle and Don facing the debuting former Junior Heavyweight Champion Mike Clancy. There would be a rare third announced match in the TV listings with Carlisle and Clancy teaming to battle the Fargos. It would also be announced during the show that Red Cloud's opponent would be the "St. Louis Rubberman" Joe Millich.

It would be noted in a Wednesday article that Clancy and James had been teaming for the past year "in the South" – so it's very likely they had faced the Fargos a few times working the regular Gulas/Welch towns. That night, there would be a change in the opener, as Millich of the St. Louis Wrestling Club would be replaced by Tennessee's Luke Fields who wrestled the Chief to a 20-minute draw. Bob Corby would get the win over Tor Yamata when the judo-master was disqualified for not breaking a hold in the third fall. In the Main Event… Things got complicated.

"Wednesday night's feature wrestling event at the Coliseum was ruled "no contest" when deputy commissioner Forrest Emery reversed referee Wayne Pate's decision.

Jackie and Don Fargo were the apparent winners of their tag match with Mike Clancy and Jesse James when Jackie pinned James with a knee drop to the stomach and a press to win the third and deciding fall.

But Emery later ruled Jackie failed to make a proper tag in entering the ring and that neither team be declared the winner."
- Evansville Courier 07/09/59

Now in the past when Forest Emery got involved in a decision, it usually meant a rematch the next week, but not this time. Instead, on Friday the Fargos would be announced as returning on July 15th, but they would be facing another heel team. Rip Hawk and a partner to be determined.

Friday's match announcement also promised a ladies match with Kay Noble vs. Penny Banner and Farmer Marlin against Chief Red Cloud.

Speaking of promised matches, the listing for *Studio Wrestling* on the 11th was intriguing. According the *Evansville Press* TV page, Hawk would face Bobby Bruns in the first bout while the Fargos would take each other on in the second match with the show wrapping up with the Fargos teaming against Hawk and Bruns. During the actual broadcast, Hawk's partner for Wednesday would be revealed as the German Eric Von Brock while Penny Banner would be replaced with Jessica Rogers in the ladies' feature. The Marlin/Red Cloud match would also be adjusted, going from a 20 minute opener to 45 minutes. By Wednesday however, it would be back to a 20 minute match with Bruns replacing Red Cloud. The story being that the Chief had been injured Saturday in Louisville and was in St. Mary's Hospital Wednesday morning being treated for a back injury. Also on Wednesday, Banner was back on the card against Noble.

Once the bell rang that night, the Coliseum would be packed to gills. In the opener, things would change once again with Farmer Marlin taking on Bill Longson and going to a 20-minute draw. The ladies match would have a substitution as well and wind up being stopped by referee Ralph Hamilton. Noble and Kay Starr would be tied at a fall apiece when Starr continued to ignore Hamilton's order to stop pulling Noble's hair. He finally called for the bell and awarded the match to Noble.

The main event fortunately had all of its scheduled combatants available. The Fargos would take the first fall when Don pinned Von Brock, while Von Brock would capture the second fall, injuring Don Fargo's back in the process. When Don could not return for the third stanza, the match would be awarded to Hawk and Von Brock.

On Thursday, Leon Balkin would reveal the next Wednesday card would be headlined by Hawk taking on Don Fargo in a one-on-one, no time limit "revenge match" with the rest of the card to be revealed later Friday. Those other matches would include Farmer Marlin and Tommy O'Toole against Wild Bill Longson and Tor Yamata. Former Big Ten wrestling champion Jim La Rock would be in the opener against an opponent to be revealed during Saturday night's *Studio Wrestling* show.

The TV listing promised Rip Hawk against Bob Corby and Farmer Marlin vs. Erik Von Brock with the four men meeting later in a tag team contest. Corby would also be announced as the opponent for the debuting LaRock during the broadcast, while Bobby Bruns would be revealed as the special referee for the Hawk/Fargo match where both combatants would put their pay for the night on the line.

LaRock, a two-time former AAU champion, would win the opener against Corby and the Marlin/O'Toole tag team would be victorious against Yamata and substitute partner Billy McDaniel.

The main event would be a wild one. Don Fargo would win the first fall at 4:10 using brother Jackie's atomic drop finisher. Hawk would even things 1:50 into the second fall with a series of flying tackles and a reverse crab submission. The third fall would be won by Hawk, but not without controversy. Bruns, the special referee, would be knocked around in the deciding frame, winding up in the floor twice. The second time he tumbled from the ring it was with Fargo on top of him two minutes in. Regular referee Wayne Pate would hit the ring and give Fargo the 20-count and award the match to Hawk.

The following Friday, Promoter Balkin would announce a rematch for July 29th, this time with two referees trying to maintain order between Hawk and Fargo. Also Tor Yamata would be joined by 245-lb countryman Kinji Shibuya to face Marlin and O'Toole. No opening match was announced but potential names floated included regulars James and Clancy as well as newcomer Jim LaRock and a man who had yet to appear in Evansville in 1959… Freddie Blassie.

As the remnants of Hurricane Debra reached the Midwest, resulting in a rainy Saturday night, the fans who braved the weather to get into the WTVW studio were drawn by the promise of matches with Tor Yamata against Eddy Davey and Rip Hawk facing off with Jim LaRock. They would also learn the Wednesday night opening match would feature Eric Von Brock against Carlos Romero. And, since his frequent tag partner would be in the building, Hawk would request that Von Brock be in his corner for the rematch with Fargo.

On the 29th, Von Brock would win the opener and the Japanese team of Yamata and Shibuya would defeat the makeshift team of Tommy O'Toole and Sammy Ford, who was replacing an absent Farmer Marlin. The main event would again end in controversy, with Don Fargo standing tall despite having his shoulders pinned for a 3-count. Rip would win the first fall at 4:30 after a back body drop while Fargo would catch Hawk with his own "atomic bomb" move to take the second fall. In the third fall, Hawk would pin Fargo, but the referee would reverse the decision and award the match to Fargo because his foot was outside the ropes during the pin.

The only reason I can guess that the match was given to Fargo rather than restarting the fall is a possible curfew for the matches. For whatever reason the decision was made, it did keep the Hawk/Fargo feud going.

On July 31st, the next Wednesday night card would be announced and Leon Balkin would unveil a packed card. A tag team main event would see Hawk and Von Brock against the Fargos plus the semi-final would have Yamata and Shibuya meeting O'Toole and LaRock. The two tag matches being billed as part of a tournament to crown new Indiana Tag Team Champions. Balkin also announced Mike Mazurki, the former football player and wrestler turned actor, would referee at least one of the bouts and single matches would see Don Fargo against Von Brock and Shibuya would be up against O'Toole. But as we know from a number of the cards that ran this month, the card is "Subject To Change."

August 1959

The 1st day of August would fall on a Saturday, but this would be one of those occasions where the *Evansville Press* TV listings would not have any matches down for that night's *Studio Wrestling* show. What we can assume is the show would be built around the Indiana Tag Championship tournament matches on Wednesday and specifically the grudge match between the team of Rip Hawk and Eric Von Brock against Jackie and Don Fargo. Depending on his availability, the local viewer might also have seen Wednesday's special referee, Mike Mazurki.

Mazurki was a Ukranian immigrant who came to the U.S. at the age of 6 and he grew up around Albany, NY. Standing at 6'5" when he graduated high school, he would play football and basketball at Manhattan College. After getting his B.A., he went onto get a law degree from Fordham. He was quoted as saying he became a professional wrestler after playing pro football because he could earn around ten times as much in the ring as he could as a lawyer. He would make his first appearance in an Evansville ring in 1938 and he'd be a regular through 1940 and then make a number of visits – often paired against Lou Thesz – between 1948 and 1952. In between his Evansville wrestling stints, he would be discovered by director Josef Von Sternberg, launching a career of playing tough guys, wrestlers and mob enforcers that would continue up to 1990, the year he passed away. Along with being in both the 1945 and 1990 DICK TRACY films, he was even featured in music videos – knocking out Rod Stewart in the 1984 clip for the song "Infatuation."

Big Mike wouldn't be the only special referee on the evening of August 5th. It would be announced that the referees for the single fall matches would be selected from the fans at ringside, which sounds like a bad idea now when the worked nature of the business is acknowledged. The thought of making a fan, who wasn't a plant, in 1959 the referee for match is borderline scary. Fortunately, this would be clarified by Tuesday that if the single matches went to the time limit without a pin or submission, three fans from ringside would be chosen to act more like boxing judges to render a decision.

On the night of the 5th, Hawk and Von Brock would advance, topping the Fargos while Yamata and Shibuya would knock off O'Toole and LaRock, guaranteeing another heel-v-heel main event on the 12th. As for the preliminaries, the fans would have to decide the winner between Don Forgo and Von Brock, with Von Brock getting the nod. In the other 15-minute single, it would be changed to LaRock vs. Yamata, with the former AAU champ given the victory via disqualification.

On Friday, Promoter Balkin would formally announce the main event of Hawk and Von Brock against Yamata and Shibuya as the tournament match to decide the "Evansville finalist" for the Indiana Tag titles. The winners would have to win another match to get a shot at the World Tag Team champions – most likely the Tennessee version of that title as the NWA did not formally recognize team champions until the 1980s when the Crockett version of the title was the only one of the multiple "World Tag" versions to still be active. Balkin would also promise former Olympic champion Jim LaRock in action on the 12th as well as some new faces.

For the second week in a row, no matches are given in Saturday's Studio Wrestling TV listing, so we can't confirm if any of those "new faces" debuted on August 8th, but more of the August 12th Coliseum card was probably revealed. Larry Cheyne, a newcomer from Detroit, would be booked to face Tommy O'Toole while LaRock's opponent would be Texan Herb Larson. There would be a hiccup with the main event, however. Von Brock reportedly complained of a sore back after the match with the Fargos on the 5th. Promoter Balkin told the local press that upon seeing his doctor in St. Joseph, MO, Von Brock was ordered to not wrestle for at least two weeks. It would be months before the man later known as Rock Hunter would return to Evansville. On Tuesday, Von Brock's replacement would be revealed as former world's champion Wild Bill Longson.

There would be more changes caused by injuries on Wednesday. Larry Cheyne would wind up beating Jim LaRock 2-falls to-1 due to O'Toole being injured Monday during the TV matches in St. Louis. With LaRock moved to the semi-main event, his spot would be assumed by Farmer Marlin who would get the victory after Larson was disqualified. As for the Tag Tournament main event – after not getting involved for the past few weeks, Deputy Athletic Commissioner Forest Emery would strike again, declaring the bout a "No Contest."

In the third fall, a free-for-all broke out between the teams with most of the action taking place on the Coliseum floor rather than the ring.

The brawl wasn't the only news Rip Hawk made on that Wednesday. The blonde bruiser who had moved to Evansville in June was announced as one of the newest competitors at a venue that would be hosting wrestling in just a few years...

"Rip Hawk, who has dominated the local wrestling scene for the past several months, will try his hand at another sport Sunday night when he is scheduled to drive in the stock car racing program at the Tri-State Speedway near Haubstadt.

Hawk, who joined the course's driver's association to gain eligibility, has driven previously in and around Albuquerque, N.M."
-Evansville Courier 08/14/59

A couple of days before the Hawk would try to make his racing debut, he would be announced to be in a return bout for Wednesday the 19th. Hawk and Longson would meet the Japanese team again, this time with no time limit and no disqualification. Hawk's day on the track was set for Sunday as to not miss the live TV at WTVW. On that Saturday night the supporting matches of a second attempt to have Larry Cheyne meet Tommy O'Toole plus Herb Larson vs. Chief Red Cloud were announced. As for Sunday's racing... Hawk would not get to take his car onto the track due to rainy conditions.

What may not have been announced in the press was what was going on with the whole Indiana State Tag Team Championship tournament angle. Rather than the winning team getting a shot at the world tag team champs, it would be announced on August 18th that now the captain of the winning team – either Hawk or Shibuya – would get a shot at five-time NWA World Champion Lou Thesz. Apparently the winning team would also still be active in the tournament whose bracket must have been the inspiration for some "tournaments" conducted by promotions in the 80s and 90s.

On that Wednesday, Red Cloud and Larson would go to the 20-minute time limit and the summer injury bug would strike again in the semi-final, as Cheyne would be scratched from the night's lineup. Instead it would be Jesse Venegas falling to Tommy O'Toole. In the main event, Hawk would get the shot at Thesz and stay alive in the "tournament" thanks to Longson's series of piledrivers on the heavyweight Shibuya.

An interesting wrinkle in the Hawk/Thesz match-up was it being promoted as the start of Thesz' push for a sixth NWA championship. If he were to get by Hawk, Thesz would then face former champ Dick Hutton with the winner to get a match with Pat O'Connor for the title.

The next Wednesday night would be booked like most NWA championship appearances with the undercard made up of three extra matches. In this case, Bill Longson in a single fall contest, a ladies match with Kathy Starr against newcomer Judy Glover and Lord Littlebrook – now billed as claimant to the midget world championship – in a single fall bout. During Saturday's TV, Longson's oponent would be revealed as Tommy O'Toole in a 20-minute match while Littlebrook would be challenged by Bull Brummel in the opener.

On the night of the 26th, Littlebrook would again defeat Brumell while O'Toole would prove to still be tough to pin down at the Coliseum, going to a draw with Longson. In the ladies match, newcomer Glover would bounce back from losing the first fall to take the last two from Starr. In the last main event for the month of August, Hawk would pin the former champion, but his old foes, referee Wayne Pate and Deputy Commissioner Emery, would reverse the decision after Emcry ruled Hawk had both feet on the bottom rope during the deciding pinfall.

The month would close with announcement of the first September card being a triple main event. The opener would be a midget tag match with Lord Littlebrook and Cowboy Bradley against Bull Brummel and Tiny Roe. Longson and O'Toole would meet again, this time with a 45 minute time limit and the final match would see Hawk getting cheers, but not against Thesz. For him to get his rematch with the former champion, he would have get past the 245-pound former Sumo Kinji Shibuya.

September 1959

At the end of August, Leon Balkin's NWA office was still going strong with blonde bad guy Rip Hawk as the primary attraction. That's not to say Hawk's heelish actions didn't have fans among the Coliseum faithful, especially among the teens in the crowd. But others who had jeered the man back in January were starting to embrace him. Thanks to moving his young family to the city in June and Balkin scheduling him against more natural heels, the rulebreaker would experience a level of popularity akin to that of future protege Ric Flair in the Carolinas or Steve Austin in the WWF prior to the double-switch against Bret Hart. Hawk would also be a draw around cities promoted by the Central States promotional alliance of Balkin, Sam Muchnick and Jim Barnett. In late August, a card headlined by Hawk challenging NWA Champion Pat O'Connor drew 14,000 in St. Louis, Muchnick's largest crowd in five years.

On September 2nd, Hawk was scheduled to face Japanese heavyweight Kinji Shibuya, who had risen to the level of #2 heel in Evansville – arguably #1 when you throw in the lingering resentment from World War II. The winner of the match would face Lou Thesz, who was pursuing his sixth NWA championship. Hawk had pinned Thesz at the Coliseum in August, but had seen the decision reversed by Deputy Athletic Commissioner Forest Emery who saw "The Hawk" using the ropes for leverage during the pin. Other matches on the 2nd would see Wild Bill Longson and Tommy O'Toole in a rematch after they wrestled to a 20 minute draw in the opening match a week prior. This time, they would be given 45 minutes and best two-of-three falls.

A midget tag bout would open things with the return of Lord Littlebrook and Cowboy Bradley against Tiny Roe and Bull Brummel.

That night, Littlebrook and Bradley would win the rematch of the tag bout that had been part of May's show at Roberts Stadium. O'Toole would drop the first fall in his match against former World's Champion Longson, but would rally to take the second and, thanks to the veteran suffering a leg injury in the second fall, the Irish babyface would win the third, getting Longson to submit 1:30 into the round. In the main event, Shibuya would take the first fall while Hawk would even it up in the second. He would still have the advantage in the third fall when his Atomic Bomb finisher would backfire. As he dove off the ropes, Hawk cracked heads with Shibuya, leading referee Ralph Hamilton to count both heels out and declare the match a "no contest."

The status of the match with Thesz – with another shot at Pat O'Connor's title at stake –would be addressed on Saturday's live *Studio Wrestling* show. Earlier in the day however, Rip Hawk's next appearance on the track would be announced.

 After his last appearance at Tri-State Speedway saw him driving his modified stock car the wrong direction, Labor Day Monday, September 7th, he would be driving a midget racer before heading to wrestle in Owensboro. On Saturday night, the rematch with Shibuya would be formally booked for Wednesday with the Thesz match no longer on the table but a meeting with O'Connor on the line as the stipulation instead. Meanwhile, Tommy O'Toole learned he would be matched with the 280-lb "Georgia Giant," Don Rocky Lee. The announced one-fall opener would be Larry Cheyne, returning from injury, to take on Chico Cortez with a special 1-hour time limit.

As for Hawk's race on Labor Day, the grappler took the #68 midget racer onto the track for some practice laps, but once the racing started, the car's engine blew while piloted by another driver, causing that driver to suffer burns to his legs when sprayed with hot oil and water. Due to the time taken to clean up the track and the lack of another ride, Rip would forgo racing and leave for his match in Owensboro. For the record, the matches at the Sportcenter on September 7th were promoted by Gulas/Welch and we know of two matches booked for that night – a singles match with Jackie Fargo facing Pat McManus and a tag contest where Hawk would be teamed with Saul Weingroff against Tex Riley and promoter Roy Welch.

As for the Wednesday night matches in Evansville, it looks to have been uneventful in the undercard, with Larry Cheyne topping Chico Cortez and O'Toole defeating Lee. In the main event, Wayne Pate was put in the rare position of helping Rip Hawk. The referee would wind up disqualifying Shibuya in the third fall when the Japanese star refused to release a chokehold on Hawk.

On Saturday night, the next Wednesday card would be revealed and the headliners would be Hawk and O'Toole meeting for the fourth time at the Coliseum. It had been a few weeks since they last met and Hawk was declared the victor due to a cut around O'Toole's eye leading to a stoppage. The midcard would see Hans Schmidt booked in Evansville for the first time in seven years to face Stan Lisowski, the kayfabe "brother" of "The Crusher" as well as being a wrestler last seen locally in 1957. The opener would have Farmer Marlin taking on Herb Larson. Wednesday's newspapers would announce a NWA Championship match on the 23rd being at stake in the main event.

When the 16th rolled around, Farmer Marlin would take the decision against Herb Larson, while Schmidt would be awarded the semi-final when Lisowski tossed the German over the top rope in the third fall. In the main event, the grudge match between the two most successful wrestlers locally would go to the blonde terror when O'Toole – who was the babyface – got himself disqualified for choking Hawk in the first fall and then dropped the second fall to the former New Mexico resident.

So the next Wednesday's main event was set. Hawk and O'Connor would meet for the first time since their St. Louis match where Hawk claimed to have won because the champ threw him over the top rope, and for the first time in Evansville since the May Stadium show. This time, they would have a 90-minute time limit to work with. The middle match would also be revealed during *Studio Wrestling* with Tommy O'Toole and Kinji Shibuya squaring off. The midget match announced on Saturday would be canceled due to other commitments, so promoter Balkin would announce a replacement ladies match on the day before with Cora Combs against Anne LaVerne. By

Wednesday, a fourth match would be added. In that opening contest, Stan Lisowski and Farmer Marlin would wrestle to a 20 minute draw. In the ladies' special bout, Combs would take the fall from LaVerne. The semi-final match would go to a third fall before referee Wayne Pate finally disqualified Shibuya for continuing to go after O'Toole's eyes. The main event would also go to a third fall, but Hawk would once again come up short. After splitting the first two falls, the local favorite would be stunned by a blow to the head and be pinned by the champ.

Saturday night the 26th, no matches would be listed for the *Studio Wrestling* show on the *Press*' TV page, which had been the norm since August. The show had a new lead-in with the Sammy Kaye big band program giving way to documentary series *The Big Picture* over the summer and *Sea Hunt* taking over the 9:30pm slot with the start of the Fall TV season. On this night, Balkin's TV risked a delayed start as ABC would air a prime time NFL game between the Browns and Steelers.

That wouldn't be the only challenge faced by the local promotion that weekend. On Sunday, WEHT – then on Channel 50 – ran a 2-page spread in the Sunday "Look" section of the *Courier and Press* plugging their Fall line-up and a contest to get people to watch the new programs. Among the promised new syndicated shows on "Living Tape" to debut on October 5th was "Wrestling." With the local NWA office contracted with WTVW, this would be an unaffiliated group moving into the market – possibly the Chicago group running the International Amphitheater that would in a few months evolve into part of the AWA. But their program was already airing on Harrisburg, IL based WSIL-TV whose coverage area bled into the western edge of the Evansville market enough that the local papers carried the station's schedule.

Folks who stayed up for the TV matches on the 26th learned that the Indiana Tag Team Tournament, although not discussed since mid August, was still going and the next elimination match would take place on the 30th with the local team of Rip Hawk and Wild Bill Longson, who was now the permanent replacement for the incapacitated Eric Von Brock, going up against the Corsica Brothers, Joe and Jean. Other Wednesday matches would be a 2-out of-3 fall midget match with Tiny Roe against Cowboy Bradley and a single-fall opener with Farmer Marlin meeting Ray Spindola.

When the 30th rolled around, Marlin would pick up the victory in the opener against the St. Louis regular Spindola. Cowboy Bradley would win the midget bout that served as the semi-main event. As for the actual main event, neither team would advance in the Indiana Tag Tournament on this night.

Few details would be offered by the local newspapers. What was reported was the match turned into a wild brawl with all four men in the ring at the same time. Not content to pound on each other, referee Ralph Hamilton was also knocked around to the point he called for the bell, leaving the match as "no contest."

The day after the matches, the public unintentionally learned a bit about the local promotion's overhead in presenting the weekly cards. At this point, Coliseum management fell to the Vanderburgh County Commissioners. At their Thursday morning meeting, the president of the local Broadway Theater League spoke requesting the rent for the non-profit's upcoming four night engagement featuring actress Ethel Berrymore be reduced to the same $90 per night rate offered to charitable organizations. The rate they had been quoted, and most likely what Leon Balkin was paying every week… $105. In 2019 values, that would be $368.

Despite kids heading back to school and those other traditional factors that always made September a difficult month for promoters, the Balkin/Hawk team continued to be big box office in Evansville. Now, the gray skies of October were approaching, bringing along with the added distractions of the Fall Festival and Jaycees' Rodeo.

WRESTLING
SPORTSCENTER
Monday, Sept. 7, 8:30 P.M.

MAIN EVENT
TEX RILEY & ROY WELCH
VS.
Rip Hawk & Sol Weingroff

JACKIE FARGO
VS.
PAT McMANUS

TICKETS ON SALE
ALL DAY MONDAY
AT SPORTSCENTER

October 1959

As the 1960 models were starting to arrive in local auto dealer showrooms and the West Side Nut Club's Fall Festival was getting underway, promoter Leon Balkin was surely celebrating what had been a banner year so far. Even more so when compared to the 1957 and 1958 seasons. Of course a drawback to this success is people seeing how you are doing and trying to move in. With *Studio Wrestling* a hit for WTVW, WEHT would be airing a wrestling show of their own, via "Living Tape" starting this month. On the positive front, a number of stars who avoided Evansville during the lean years were now eager to work for Leon on Wednesday nights. One of those stars was the high-flying Antonio "Argentine" Rocca.

Rocca was one of the flashiest stars of the early-television wrestling boom. Wrestling barefoot, he electrified audiences with his arsenal of dropkicks, flying scissors and overall agility. In 1959, he would take over the Madison Square Garden wrestling office with Jack Pfefer, but still manage to take his first Evansville booking since 1952 to open the month of October. Balkin would issue the press release on October 2nd, noting Rocca had drawn $300,000 over six appearances at the Garden during its 1959 wrestling season and that he would likely face Tommy O'Toole on Wednesday. The rematch between the Hawk/Longson team and the Corsica Brothers following the September 30th "no contest" would also be revealed. On Saturday night during *Studio Wrestling*, an opening match between Farmer Marlin and Rocca stablemate Harry Lewis would be revealed.

While Rocca was being pushed as the primary attraction for October 7th, Lewis would not see much benefit to being associated with the star. The Farmer would make Lewis submit 9:30 into their 30-minute opener. O'Toole continued to show a rougher attitude as he would be disqualified in the first fall of the feature with Rocca. The Argentine would take the match in straight falls, using a back-breaker to dispatch O'Toole in the second round. And in the Main Event, Hawk would remind the local fans who had found themselves pulling for the blonde bomber that he was not one of the good guys. The Corsica Brothers would "advance" in the Indiana Tag Tournament thanks to a conflict developing between Rip and Wild Bill. During the match, the pair started to appear angry with each other and began refusing to tag their partner. In the third fall, Hawk would get fed up and leave the ring, going to the dressing room. Reports are unclear if he was the legal man and was counted out or if this was a quirk of the rules in the 1950s where if one tag partner could not, or would not in this case, continue the match, their opponents would be awarded the victory.

With both the "Indiana Tag Tournament" storyline and his partnership with former champ Longson effectively ended, Rip Hawk was now freed up for singles matches again. One would think a grudge match between Hawk and Longson would be the logical main event for the next week. But instead Hawk would be scheduled to meet Corsica Joe and Leon Balkin would up the stakes, promising a match with Lou Thesz if Joe could topple the Hawk. Meanwhile

Corsica Jean would be scheduled against Larry Cheyne for Wednesday and the opener would be set with Luigi Mascera of Mexico City (actually of Montreal) taking on Chuck Grant.

It appears Grant and Cheyne would not make it to Evansville on that Wednesday. The single-fall opener would change to Herb Larson against Charlie Garza with Larson getting the win. Mascera would be moved into the mid-card spot against Corsica Jean, but would lose the two-out of-three fall match. Their conflict wouldn't end with the final fall, however. In the main event, Hawk and Corsica Joe were even at a fall apiece when Joe was joined by his younger brother for the third and Jean started helping attack the local star when Joe had the referee distracted. This would draw out Mascera from the dressing room and as the match disintegrated into a melee, the referee would final have enough and award the match to Hawk by disqualification.

With the DQ figuring into the decision, Corsica Joe claimed that he was truly the victor, and demanded a return match against Hawk on October 21st with no time limit. Corsica Jean would make the Evansville trip with his brother to once again wrestle Maceara in the semi-main event, but was warned in advance by Deputy Athletic Commissioner Emery to stay away from the ring during the main event. For the opener, Jesse James would make his first trip back to town since the summer to battle Mark Starr.

 On that Wednesday, Starr and James would go to a time limit draw to start the night and Mascera would avenge his loss of a week earlier by taking the second and third falls of the semi-final match, the third fall pin coming after Corsica Jean struck his head on the turnbuckle which left him unable to continue. In the main event, Corsica Joe's temper cost him the match, as his refusal to back up and let Hawk re-enter the ring forced referee Wayne Pate to call for a disqualification and award the first fall to Hawk. Working from that advantage, Hawk would only need a little over five minutes to get a pin on Joe following a standing back body drop.

During October, the good name of professional wrestling was often being invoked in relation to one of the major stories of the day – the 1959 Quiz Show Scandal.

In the late 50s, one of the few formats that even remotely challenged Westerns for domination on network television were the quiz shows like 21, Dotto and others. By the fall, all were facing scrutiny after it was revealed that producers were passing along answers to the contestants they wanted to win. One U.S. Representative who demanded oversight on programming by both the FCC and FTC was rebuffed by FTC chairman Earl Kintner who argued imposing complete censorship of all entertainment could see his commission policing wrestling matches.

Of course the $21,000 question in the city of Evansville on the 23rd of October was "Who does Rip Hawk face next?" On that Friday, Balkin would reveal the next Wednesday night main event as Hawk vs. Canadian Luigi Mascera, the man who two weeks prior came to his aid against the Corsica brothers, while the undercard would be announced as Kay Noble and Loraine Johnson meeting again in an

Evansville ring and the return of former Olympian Jim LaRock against an opponent to be named on Saturday night's TV. That announced opponent for the 28th would be Carlos Rodriguez

As it would turn out, once again, the main event would be the only advertised match to actually take place. LaRock would instead face Herb Larson in the opener and the victory went to the former AAU champion. In the special women's bout, Johnson would be replaced by Ella Waldek, who would be disqualified giving Kay Noble a win. In the final, Hawk and Mascera would go all three falls, Hawk taking the first after a series of knee drops to the Canadian's throat and Mascera using a reverse crab to win the second. Hawk would take the third fall after a series of "atom bombs."

Halloween night would be the month's final edition of *Studio Wrestling* and set up the November 4th card and the direction of the local promotion for the rest of the year by featuring a wild brawl between Hawk and LaRock.

Frog and Hawk: Smiley Burnette (left) known as "Frog" to Western fans, shows his versatility Sunday to Rip Hawk, a villain in pro wrestling, by applying a sort of headlock. Burnette will be the star attraction at the Jaycees Rodeo Thursday through Sunday at the Stadium. Hawk has accepted a Jaycee challenge to ride a bucking bronco at the rodeo. Burnette seems to have got his hold mixed up. He's biting the hand that feeds him. The former sidekick of Gene Autry arrived here Sunday and will make several advance appearances before the rodeo opens.

November 1959

From January to October of 1959, Rip Hawk was not only Public Enemy #1 in the eyes of the Evansville wrestling fans, but he was arguably also the region's top box office attraction. If the NWA Champion came to town, he was facing The Hawk. But much as Jerry Jarrett would be concerned with as Jerry Lawler chased the NWA and AWA titles in the 70s and 80s, promoter Leon Balkin had to be asking himself how many times can your top local star come up short in the title hunt before the fans stop believing there's a chance?

As November rolled in, Rip Hawk was still the king of the Coliseum. The only one-on-one matches he had lost in the ring were to NWA kingpin Pat O'Connor, and O'Connor was due back in town soon as the annual Courier Christmas Fund show had been headlined by the NWA Champion the past few years.

As for the rest of the local regulars, Tommy O'Toole was last seen on October 7th when he dropped two straight falls to a visiting Antonio Rocca. Perhaps, that's just as well as prior to that match he had been dominated by both Hawk and Kinji Shibuya. He had been the closest thing to a top regular babyface through the year, but based on his recent record he would likely not be taken seriously as a threat to the World Champion by the fans. But another young man who had made some appearances in the summer of '59 – despite having lost some of those matches – was back in the area and had the credentials to be the "white hat" hero to counter the blonde outlaw who had taken over the town.

James C. LaRock was born in New York on September 3, 1924. Graduating high school in 1942, he went straight into the Army, earning a European-African Middle Eastern Campaign medal among others during WWII. After the war, he pursued amateur wrestling, becoming national YMCA champion and a two-time AAU champion wrestling for Ithaca College. In 1952, He would be defeated by eventual gold medalist Bill Smith at the meet to decide that year's Olympic team. While he lost, LaRock would go to Helsinki as an alternate; leading to Balkin's stretching of the truth as he built up LaRock to the press as a "former Olympic champion." After getting his Master of Science degree in 1952, he turned down a coaching offer to instead turn pro, debuting for promoter Al Haft in 1954. By 1958, he would be recognized as the NWA U.S. Junior Heavyweight champ in Oklahoma and have the distinction of wrestling in the first match to air as part of St. Louis' long running *Wrestling From the Chase* TV show.

It would be another TV show, the local *Studio Wrestling*, where LaRock would make his first real impact in Evansville, as newspaper reports would mention the Halloween night brawl between LaRock and Hawk during the show that led to Wednesday night's main event. The pair would be booked for 2-out of-3 falls and a one hour time limit. Fans would also be promised Central States women's champion Loraine Johnson defending against Gloria Barratini, who had entered the ring after giving up a career in opera. Tommy O'Toole would return to the River City as well to take on debuting Cuban heavyweight Juan Ramirez in the 20-minute opener.

When November 4th rolled around, the substitution bug would strike again. Ramirez would no-show, replaced by Herb Larson who would then be defeated by O'Toole. And wherever the 230-lb Cuban was, perhaps he was joined by a former opera singer, as Miss Barratini would be replaced by Millie Stafford. Stafford would also fall to the scheduled opponent who made it to the Coliseum, as Johnson would take two of the three falls. In the main event, the unthinkable happened. Rip Hawk would be defeated by someone other than the NWA champ.

The first fall would go to Hawk, but not easily. It would be a hard fought 19 minutes before he would catch the former AAU champion with his "atom bomb" move from the turnbuckle. After the break, LaRock would use his mat skills to wear down the blonde bomber and force a submission with an abdominal stretch at the 10:00 mark. The third fall would be awarded to LaRock when Hawk did not answer the bell. After 11 months, the unstoppable villain had been vanquished, if only for a night, and Evansville may have found a new hero.

On Friday, promoter Balkin would announce a rematch between the two for the 11th. This card would once again feature the mixed tag match with midget men and lady wrestlers as the semi-main feature match. This time, Cowboy Bradley paired with Princess Tona Tomah against Tiny Roe and Kathy Starr with either Tommy O'Toole or Luigi Mascera in the opening one-fall contest. On Saturday's TV, it would be announced that O'Toole would open the night against Carlos Rodriguez with a 30-minute time limit. Fans would also learn of the special stipulations for Wednesday's main event. Hawk would be revealed as having asked for the rematch… but only if LaRock promised to not use the abdominal stretch. LaRock agreed on the condition Hawk not use his "atom bomb" as well.

The unusual stipulation may have been to counteract the local promotion's new "competition." We mentioned last week that WEHT had added a pro wrestling show on videotape to their schedule. What we didn't mention was *when* it was scheduled…

Wednesday nights at 10:20pm.

In theory, about the time the matches would be getting over at the Coliseum. The night of the 11th, the TV listing promised the Tolos Brothers vs. the team of Sammy Berg and Emile Dupree, Killer Kowalski against Maurice LaPointe and Frank Scarpa meeting Mike Higgins. In discussing this TV listing with wrestling historians, the consensus is Channel 50's program was the product of one of the northeastern promoters – most likely Boston or Washington D.C.

Thursday morning would see a major announcement made, but before it came the Wednesday night matches where the fans would see Tommy O'Toole use a flying head scissors to subdue Carlos Rodriguez in 16:00. In the mixed tag match, the babyface team of the Cowboy and Indian Princess would get the victory. Then came the main event with Hawk taking the first fall in 12:00 after a back body drop. The Olympic alternate would only need 3 minutes to capture the second fall, converting a cradle into a reverse crab. The third fall would only last 6:30 before the referee stopped the match due to Hawk using the "atom bomb" move that he agreed was barred on this night. Thanks to a disqualification, LaRock was the victor and the next morning, he would learn the spoils. Thursday's report of the results would include the announcement by Leon Balkin that the win earned LaRock the next shot at Pat O'Connor's title in Evansville, taking place on November 18th.

On Saturday's TV, the full card would be revealed with Tommy O'Toole scheduled in the opener with Juan Ramirez announced to try again to make his Evansville debut. A 2-of-3 fall ladies match with Princess Tona Tomah vs. Millie Stafford would also be featured while Rip Hawk would be relegated to the semi-main against local hand Farmer Marlin. Of course, the card was subject to change and by Tuesday it would do just that.

Ramirez would reportedly cancel again on Balkin and O'Toole would be shifted to the semi-main event, teaming with Marlin against Hawk and Wild Bill Longson who would be paired together for the first time since an argument between the heels led to Hawk leaving the ring for the dressing room and their elimination from the Indiana Tag Team tournament.

With the champion in town, WEHT's listing for videotaped wrestling on the 18th did not name any matches, which surely helped Balkin's disposition as the fans turned out to the Coliseum. In the opener, Princess Tomah would top Millie Stafford. In a surprise change, Farmer Marlin would be replaced by Juan Ramirez as O'Toole's partner, but they would still drop two falls to the reconciled Longson and Hawk. In the main event, the fans were treated to a classic.

O'Connor would hold onto the NWA championship, but LaRock took him to the limit. The champion would need 35:30 to capture the first fall with a reverse crab, but five minutes into the second fall LaRock would catch O'Connor in his abdominal stretch and cinch it in to get a submission after five minutes. Neither man would gain the advantage in the remaining 19-plus minutes, leaving the match as a draw and LaRock as the city's new top babyface.

It helped that LaRock wrestled in his Team USA singlet and came to the ring in the Olympic team warm-up jacket. While he was only an alternate, that combined with his legitimate amateur resume let promoter Balkin get away with billing the New Yorker as an Olympic champion, though LaRock was open in interviews about not getting the opportunity to wrestle in Finland back in 1952.

While LaRock was over, Balkin was taking no chances on his hero status fading before the rematch with O'Connor. For Wednesday the 25th, Tor Yamata would be brought back to Evansville after several months absence. The undercard would be scheduled to feature Tommy O'Toole against Georgia's Big Don "Rocky" Lee in a rematch from earlier in the year and an opener of Karl Kowalski, last seen in an Evansville ring in 1955, facing the debuting Al Medina.

On that night, Kowalski would defeat Medina in 13:00, while O'Toole would get his first loss since returning earlier in the month, dropping 2 of the 3 falls to the 300-pounder from Georgia. In the main event, LaRock would dispatch Yamata rather quickly in straight falls. He would get the initial fall when Yamata was disqualified after only

4:00. After the break, the shooter from Ithica would cinch in the abdominal stretch within 3 minutes of the second fall to gain the victory.

Notably absent from Wednesday's card was Rip Hawk. While he was a major star for the St. Louis office and more than likely booked elsewhere, this was also fortunate in the effort to build up LaRock. Hawk's living in Evansville and 11-month run on TV and at the Coliseum had given him a degree of popularity despite his heelish actions in the ring. Without Hawk in the building, all the attention would be on LaRock making short work of the Japanese villain.

Friday morning, LaRock's next challenge would be revealed as Don "Rocky" Lee. The premise in setting up the match being Lee's claim that his 300-pound girth would counter LaRock's abdominal stretch. No other matches would be announced prior to Saturday's *Studio Wrestling* show, but Balkin did say Karl Kowalski would be back and that he was attempting to sign Bobby Managoff to come in. But as we've noted... Card Subject To Change.

By Sunday, the entire card had been shuffled, likely due to events of the Saturday night TV. Kowalski would be in the opener against Hal Martin with a rare one hour time limit. Don "Rocky" Lee was still booked to appear, but the now 315-pounder (as of the 11/29 newspaper) would be in the semi-main event against the 545 pound "Mighty Jumbo" and his bone-crushing flying splash. With Lee moved out of the main event, Rip Hawk would move in with the idea being that if Hawk could finally beat LaRock, he would get the next title shot at the Coliseum against O'Connor in December.

The Killer Returns: Wladek Kowalski, Polish giant of Detroit nativity, returns to the Coliseum Wednesday night after a five-year absence. He is known as "The Killer" in heavyweight wrestling circles. His opponent will be Tommy O'Toole, a personable Irishman.

December 1959

On the night of December 2nd, fans would turn out for a card so big, the ring had to be reinforced.

Literally.

With the two men in the semi-final weighing in at close to a combined 900 pounds, it needed to be. But the build to the next visit by NWA champion Pat O'Connor was now underway and the next title shot would go to either Rip Hawk, who had dominated the Evansville scene since showing up on *Studio Wrestling* almost a year prior, and Jim LaRock, an amateur champion who had been an alternate for the 1952 US Olympic wrestling team.

The first Wednesday of December began with Karl Kowalski defeating Howard Martin and Don "Rocky" Lee managing to whip the larger Mighty Jumbo in a rare one-fall semifinal. And in the main event, Hawk and LaRock would give the Coliseum audience a show. Hawk would take the first fall after dropping the AAU champion with three back body drops to set up a pin. LaRock evened things up in the second, catching the New Mexico native in his abdominal stretch. As the third fall time ticked away, Hawk would wear down LaRock enough that he was set up for the "atom bomb," but as the blonde ruffian was perched on the top turnbuckle, he lost his footing and fell to the floor. The referee saw him outside the ring and began his 20-count. The bell rang and LaRock's arm was raised as the once-dominating heel lay in the aisle trying to regain his senses.

Five weeks in a row and LaRock had not been defeated at the Coliseum and he had continued the streak on Saturday nights having won five straight matches on *Studio Wrestling*. For December 9th, promoter Balkin opted to try again with the LaRock/Rocky Lee match he originally announced for the 2nd. The return of former National Wrestling Association champion Bobby Managoff hinted for the 2nd would actually be announced for the 9th, bringing him back for the first time in two years to battle Rip Hawk. The man who defeated Managoff for the old NWA championship, Wild Bill Longson, would face Don McClarity in the opener.

Those pesky card changes would strike again on Wednesday, a both Longson and Managoff would miss the show. Herb Larson would step in and wrestle Don McClarity to a 30-minute draw. Managoff's replacement against Rip Hawk would be Eddie Davie. While the name Eddie Davie might not be familiar, he was and would be a somewhat frequent visitor to Evansville under the name "Pat Malone" and under the mask of "The Green Shadow" he would be the partner of a young Jerry Lawler when the future "King" made his first appearance in the city. Davie/Malone would make it a match, losing the first fall to a back body drop at the 15:00 mark and recovering to nail Hawk with a drop kick en route to winning the second at 2:40. Hawk would get back on the winning track when Davie was counted out in the third and deciding fall.

In the main event, LaRock would remain unbeaten for the sixth straight week, disposing of his plus-sized opponent in straight falls. Lee did not help himself in the match, getting disqualified at 18:00 into the first fall for choking. When they returned to the ring for the second fall, LaRock wasted little time proving he could lock his abdominal stretch onto a larger man, forcing a submission at 2:45. With the win, his rematch with O'Connor at the next week's *Evansville Courier* Christmas Fund benefit card was secured. On Thursday, Balkin would confirm Rip Hawk, Loraine Johnson and – this time for sure – Bobby Managoff would be at the Coliseum on December 16th.

On Friday, the full card would be announced. Tommy O'Toole would get a place on the card, facing one of the stars of the wrestling show on WEHT... Wladek "Killer" Kowalski. Kowalski, who most modern fans know as the man who trained HHH and Chyna, was one of the biggest ring villains of the 60s and 70s and would be coming to Evansville for the first time since 1954. Next up, Loraine Johnson was scheduled to meet Cora Combs. The undercard to O'Connor/LaRock II would be rounded out by a tag match. Rip Hawk and the now "Cowboy" Rocky Lee would face Managoff and Don McClarity.

The week leading up to the card of December 16th would see a charm offensive not unlike the push going into the Stadium event the prior spring. The *Evansville Courier*, which tended to cover the local NWA office at arm's length and raised eyebrows compared to the more in depth coverage by the afternoon *Evansville Press*, would give the show benefiting their charity the hard sell with articles through the week and a flattering profile of challenger LaRock by columnist Daniel Scism. In a callback to the promotion done around town in the 1930s, LaRock would hold a public workout the night before the championship match at the YMCA downtown. For added community goodwill, the former AAU champion would be offering instruction to some of the youths taking part in the Y's wrestling program.

We'd also see ticket prices listed for the first time since the Stadium show. Ringside seats for the 16th would be $2.40 each – That would be $20.86 in 2019. General admission seats were $1, or $8.69 in today's dollars and kids were admitted for 50 cents. ($4.35 today)

Around 2,300 would turn out on the 16th and would be treated to a hot opening tag match with Hawk capturing the first fall on McClarity after 11:00 of action with a pair of back body drops. Rip's team would be disqualified in the second after 7:20 when the big Cowboy Lee did not break a choke on Managoff before the referee finished his count. The 315-pounder redeemed himself in the third fall, catching McClarity with a flying leap and pin at 6:15.

Next would be the ladies with Sam Muchnick's Loraine Johnson against Cora Combs who was a frequent attraction for Gulas/Welch. They too would go three falls – Johnson taking the first with a back breaker to a press at 7:45. Combs would bounce back at 4:15 of the second with a reverse crab. The Central States women's champ would take the decision after capturing Combs with a flying scissors at 4:00 into the third.

The semi-main event would be a single fall contest and, in light of Kowalski's home promotion being featured on a competing television station to the one hosting the local show, a difficult one for Leon Balkin to book. "Killer" Kowalski would mark his return to Evansville by forcing Tommy O'Toole to quit due to the pressure of his claw hold after 8:45.

Then in the main event, after the announcement of the Courier Charities receiving $720 from the gate receipts, Jim LaRock would get off to a roaring start, grappling with the champ until he caught O'Connor in the abdominal stretch and making him submit at the 22 minute mark. Following the break, LaRock would be in control – repeatedly nailing O'Connor with flying tackles until the champion ducked and LaRock flew into the ropes, getting his neck caught between the second and top ropes. As he tried to free himself, referee Wayne Pate began his count, reaching 20 while the local favorite still dangled outside the ring. As a result of getting his neck tangled in the ropes, LaRock was unable to answer the bell for the third fall and, once again, Pat O'Connor would escape the Coliseum with the NWA crown still his.

With the holidays, Leon Balkin would choose to not hold matches on December 23rd and instead build toward December 30th. On the 23rd, the promoter would announce that Hawk and Lee would again be teamed against opponents to be determined. He also revealed some familiar faces would be returning. Chick Garibaldi and Erik Von Brock, both who had not been seen in months would be back as would Sammy Ford and Johnny "Ace" Weaver – whose name had been mentioned as a possible talent for cards through the year – would finally be making his local debut. The actual matches as of the conclusion of the

Studio Wrestling show would be "Handsome" Sammy Ford opening against Carlos Rodriguez followed by Von Brock against Weaver. The main event would almost be a throwback to the beginning of the year as Hawk and Lee would meet the team of Garibaldi and O'Toole.

As had been the case for much of the second half of 1959, the card was subject to change. On the December 30th, "Handsome Sammy" was nowhere to be seen. Instead, Don McClarity picked up his first win in Evansville topping Rodriguez. Johnny Weaver, who would go onto become an icon in the Carolinas in the 60s and 70s, would take two from the returning Von Brock. Weaver won the first fall with a leg lock in 14:45, but be pinned by the future Rock Hunter after 9:30 in the second fall. The "German" villain would be disqualified in the final stanza to give Weaver the win. The main event grudge match would see Lee replaced due to illness with Bill Longson. Chick Garibaldi would take the first fall of the grudge match pnning Hawk at 10:50. At 11:15 into the second, Hawk would return the favor after a knee drop. With the falls even, it would wind up being O'Toole and Longson deciding the match, with O'Toole – the good soldier babyface who had been thrown in against the national stars who were passing through the city – catching the former world champion with a flying body press after 2:50 to get the three count and win the final match in Evansville for 1959.

This match may also have set up the start of 1960 as well. The main event for January's first card: Rip Hawk vs. Wild Bill Longson.

ANALYSIS

Having grown up on the Tennessee-inspired product of Jerry Jarrett's Memphis promotion and the Poffo's ICW, taking an in-depth look at what was running in 1959 was much more enlightening than I expected going in. When all I was going from was the list of results, I was impressed by the familiar names that passed through that year – Rocca, Gorgeous George and Killer Kowaslski are names that jump out at you, even when they are only doing single shots, and if you are a wrestling fan in this region who doesn't know Jackie and Don Fargo, you're not as hardcore of a fan as you thought. Once I was able to dig deeper though, I felt like I had some more insight into things like why the business died off only a few years later, why the WWA was not able to gain any traction in 1968 and why the Jarretts were able to make it work for the better part of a 25 year period.

I could be wrong, but I get the impression that Balkin's office was kind of an anomaly among NWA territories, even for its time. It was ostensibly affiliated with the St. Louis office of Sam Muchnick, but as I researched the individual wrestlers that came through, it appears two-thirds of the talent Balkin used came from the Gulas/Welch Nashville office. I found this surprising since this was after the brief season that he had formally aligned Evansville with Nashville and he later would be quoted as saying he believed Nick Gulas had tried to run him out of business. But, while Balkin may not have liked doing business with Nashville – or more specifically, with Gulas – the mix of talent and styles that turned things around for him in 1959 was not unlike the formula that would be successful in the 70s and into the 80s for the Jarretts.

- A Strong Television Product – This goes without saying. This is the "face" of the promotion. Memphis, Georgia/World Championship Wrestling on WTBS, Mid-South, all the way up to WCW Monday Nitro… When a promotion's television is running on all cylinders, even if the behind the scenes situation is less than perfect, the promotion will be perceived to be at its peak. By 1959, the *Studio Wrestling* show had been on for a couple of years and Balkin had a sense of what was going to work and what he could present for free and still get people to pay their $2.40 every Wednesday.

- A Charismatic Heel – The "cool heel" is not a new creation. I would argue that Rip Hawk was the prototype as much as Sputnik Monroe. Buddy Rogers and Gorgeous George were charismatic, generated heat and had their followings, but Hawk and Monroe had something more. They made a connection. Even though they were the bad guy, they had something that you as a fan related to, sometimes more than you related to the guy you were supposed to cheer. Ric Flair's connection to the Carolinas began when he was brought in as Hawk's cousin. Jerry Lawler spent the better part of the 80s as a babyface when he returned from his broken leg, but before the injury he was the smartass cool heel.

- The Charismatic But Sincere Babyface – Okay, this in my opinion is where Balkin suffered until the end of the year. Unfortunately, no footage of the Evansville TV exists and little to no footage of many regular Evansville workers from other territories is out there. As I went through the various news articles from the year – previews, results and the occasional feature column – the only personality that came through in print was Hawk. I can only imagine how he must have steamrolled Tommy O'Toole or Chick Garibaldi in the TV studio. The fact that he was in the mix for as much of the year as he was speaks to how genuinely over O'Toole must have been, but there is a distinct difference between his build up and what was done with Jim LaRock. LaRock was the one local babyface that Hawk could not beat in 1959. Unfortunately, he was gone from Evansville by the summer of 1960 and out of the business by 1962, otherwise Hawk/LaRock might have been remembered like Lawler/Dundee.

But for the positives, there are a few negative aspects that jumped out at me and make 1959 being such a strong year for Balkin kind of surprising.

- Gimmick Features – Granted my perspective is skewed from seeing all the previews and results of the cards together and not spread out over a year's time with context, but how many times can you bring in the midgets? Perhaps Balkin and Clayton Littlebrook had a longstanding friendship that figured into it, but practically every month Evansville would see Littlebrook against Bull Brummel, Cowboy Bradley against Tiny Roe or the team of Littlebrook and Bradley against Brummell and Roe – always with the babyfaces (Littlebrook and Bradley) going over. Maybe it wasn't as noticeable in real time, but in black and white it makes me cringe. Balkin brought the ladies in much more than a lot of promoters might have, but while they were booked almost as much as the Littlebrook crew, there was more variety in match-ups.

- Card Subject To Change – I don't hold Balkin as responsible for this issue as I do the gimmick feature matches. Using the same 4 little people was a choice on his part, where somebody not getting to Evansville on time was often out of his hands. There were even examples in 1959 of him putting card changes in the afternoon paper on Wednesday if he found out in time. That said, From the Stadium show when the two combatants from the ladies match were no shows to the end of the year, it seemed like every other week at least two of the three matches on a Wednesday night card would have substitutions.

Overall, the mix of the St Louis scientific wrestling and wild Tennessee brawling styles were perfect for Evansville fans. The irony that the brawling heel Hawk was a St. Louis guy and would be the top guy for the bulk of this year then would continue to be in the main event mix up to the Indianapolis office exerting their control seems perfect. I only wish some kinescopes of *Studio Wrestling* existed where we could see things like the Hawk/LaRock brawl and the night Hawk was knocked out by Farmer Marlin. It sounds like it was as wild and wooly as the Memphis show would be a few years later.

BLONDE AND boisterous Lorraine Johnson will tie knots with Kay Noble in one of the featured matches on the Press Charity wrestling show Wednesday night at The Stadium. Prety Lorraine is one of he nattion's foremost lady grapplers and is a member of the world champion ladies tag team.

1959 COLISEUM RESULTS

The following are results from the matches at the Soldiers & Sailors Memorial Coliseum and Roberts Stadium only. Should full reports of the WTVW *Studio Wrestling* program be found, the records will be amended.

1. Rip Hawk 26-13-8

2. Tommy O'Toole 12-12-10

3. "Farmer" Don Marlin 11-4-2

4. Jim LaRock 8-3-1

5. Eric Von Brock 7-5-1

6. Pat O'Connor 6-0-2

7. Lord Clayton Littlebrook 6-0-0

8. Chick Garibaldi 5-6-5

9. Jesse James 5-6-2

10. Don Fargo 5-4-1

11. Cowboy Bradley 5-0-0

12. Bobby Bruns 4-2-0

13. "Wild" Bill Longson 4-5-7

14. Jackie Fargo 4-2-1

53. Dick Beyer 0-1-0

54. Al Green 0-1-0

55. Joey Maxim 0-1-0

56. Jerry Miller 0-1-0

57. Lou Klein 0-1-0

58. China Mira 0-1-0

59. Tex Riley 0-1-0

60. Jack McCarthy 0-1-0

61. Bob Green 0-1-0

62. Penny Banner 0-1-0

63. Mighty Atlas 0-1-0

64. Billy Scharbet 0-1-0

65. Tito Romero 0-1-0

66. Billy McDaniel 0-1-0

67. Chris Belkas 0-1-0

68. Pat Fraley 0-1-0

69. Gorgeous George 0-1-0

70. Charlie Kean 0-1-0

71. Carlos Romero 0-1-0

72. Jesse Venegas 0-1-0

73. Anne LaVerne 0-1-0

74. Ray Spindola 0-1-0

75. Harry Lewis 0-1-0

76. Charlie Garza 0-1-0

77. Ella Waldek 0-1-0

78. Juan Ramirez 0-1-0

79. Al Medina 0-1-0

80. Hal (Howard) Martin 0-1-0

81. Mighty Jumbo 0-1-0

82. Bobby Mannagoff 0-1-0

83. Eddie Davie (Pat Malone)........................... 0-1-0

84. Dick Hutton 0-2-0

85. Sammy Ford 0-2-0

86. Carlos Rodriguez 0-2-0

87. Millie Stafford 0-2-0

88. Fuzzy Cupid 0-2-0

89. Kathy (Kay) Starr 0-4-1

90. Adrian Baillargeon 0-4-0

91. Tiny Roe 0-5-0

92. Bull Brummell 0-6-0

Wrestlers who were announced to appear but would not wrestle at the Coliseum during 1959 included Joe McCarthy, Red McIntyre, Chuck Grant, Gloria Barratini and Joe Millich. Millich was listed for television appearances as were Bob Carlisle and "Wild" Red Roberts.